Hearing Love

Charlier "Char" Reid

Copyright 2016

By

Charlier "Char" Reid

ISBN 978-0-9972816-5-1

Soft Cover

All rights reserved

No part of this book may be reproduced or transmitted in any form or by any means, electronic or mechanical, including photocopying, recording, or by any information storage and retrieval systems, without permission in writing from the copyright owner.

This book was printed in the United States of America.

To order additional copies of this book contact

Charlier "Char" Reid - crhearinglove@gmail.com

Facebook Page – **The Hearing Love Community**

Order online

@

Amazon.com

Meet Char

Charlier "Char" Reid is described by her family and friends as a "warm cup of coffee."

Her infectious, approachable nature exemplifies a true representation of the kindness of the heart of God. Her authentic, nurturing character is wrapped up in her comforting hugs and loving affirmations. Her greatest joy is being a loving Mama to her seven (7) children, their spouses, and being 'Mum-Mum' to all of her amazing grandchildren, and is honored to be known as, "Mama Char." to many.

Doing what she was born to do, Char and her husband, Pastor Rod, have served God together for over 35 years. They pastor Victory Christian Fellowship Church in Georgetown, South Carolina.

Char enjoys pouring out her life-lessons learned from marriage, motherhood and ministry. Her greatest passion is spending time alone with God. She cherishes receiving His love and giving it away.

DEDICATION

To my sweet husband, my best friend, my love, Rod:

Without your encouragement, this book would not have come to be. Thank you for every time you inspired me to keep going. Your help and support have been such a gift. I do love you so.

To my amazing children…Joel, Jacob, Joy, Julia, Janna, Janel and Jordan:

I am also thankful for you! To all of your spouses, my grandchildren, great-grandchildren and all of the generations to come: It is truly an honor to be your Mama, your Mother-in-Law, and your Mum-Mum. It is also an honor to dedicate this book of devotions to you all.

There are many, many things I desire for each of you. Many prayers have been spoken for each one, but none more than believing you will know God and hear His voice very clearly when He speaks His love to you. You all have given my life great meaning. I see His love in your eyes and feel Him in your touch. You will always be my inspiration and my "why." I love you all with a very deep, heartfelt love from the depth of my soul. I love being your Mama!

To my God: I fall in love with everything about You every day.

ACKNOWLEDGEMENTS

-_To my oldest son, Joel: Thank you for the title, Hearing Love. It is so special for so many reasons._

-_To my Daddy, Charlie Gilbert, who helped make this publication possible. I love you and miss you, Daddy. I wish you could have seen this dream come true for me._

-_To my Mother, Dorothy Peppers, for helping me with Titles for the Journals._

-_To my husband, Rod, who helped me with all our Scripture references for each one._

-_To Jordan Claire Presley and Crystal Franklin, my editors and friends! You both are amazing!!_

-_To Roy and Amy Harris, my Publisher: Thank you for helping me with this special project. You've been so gentle and kind._

God bless each one of you for the great love and support you have given so freely to me. Thank you again. I love you all.

ABOUT THE COVER

While sitting on the shore at the Sea of Galilee, my heart was overwhelmed with feelings I have never experienced before. I began gazing at this beautiful territory where the Lover of My Soul's life on Earth had been spent. So small…so beautiful. I pictured His feet walking this very shore. I could hear His Disciples laughter as they rode in with Peter when the boat was loaded with fish. I could feel His Presence. As I sat I asked the question, "Why here Jesus? How was it that from here you would choose to change the world?" Clearly He said, "Because I knew there were 11 faithful guys who would take my light into this dark world that needed me and would not stop until they had spread it so far and so wide that it would reach all the way to you!" I can't explain how I felt in that moment. A very strong burst of love ran through my whole being. With tears flowing down my face, I looked down and there at my feet was a perfect heart-shaped rock. As if we were the only ones alive at that moment, He said, "I love you!". I reached down and picked up the sticky note from heaven, the large Rock on the cover, and whispered back, "I love you too, Jesus!". I have learned to allow him to speak His love to me in the small ways. I have grown to notice His kindnesses all around me. I have realized that hearing love is a song that never stops singing, and that seeing love is my choice. So, with eyes and ears wide open, every moment is filled with God, because God is love. Today, I have a container of heart-shaped rocks and shells. They come from as far as Hawaii to right here at home. They are my collection of love notes and special moments from Him.

INTRODUCTION

Have you ever felt God's promptings? Are there moments when it seems there is a voice inside leading you in what to do next? Have you ever asked God a question and thought you were pretty sure you heard Him give you the answer? Me too!

This book is my accounts of quiet listening while alone in His Presence.

Finding quiet time to listen to God in my life has been a great challenge. With a Pastor husband, seven (7) children, home-schooling, laundry, food, friends, etc. (you get the picture?), life has been very, very busy. I can recall telling Rod, my husband, as he was leaving to go to his office to spend time with God, to "Tell Jesus I said hello! Tell Him I promise to get with Him soon!" It was a joke about how busy I was at the time, but actually it was a heart crying out for even a few moments alone in His Presence…just the two of us. Me, pouring out my heart to Him, and Him, pouring out His love to me. My "Be Still and Know that I am God" moments.

Well, as time marched on and children grew

up and left home, the silence I longed for came.

"Wait! Come back! I'm not done raising you, yet! There is more I want you to know. There is more I want to make sure you will never forget." I realize that the thing I wanted more than anything in this world was to know that they knew the voice of God when He speaks to them…to know that any situation they would ever face, God has the answer. His Word is what will carry them into the plans that He has for them. I realized I have had many of my own opinions and a lot of advice that may have been good, but none of it compares to the ability to sense and know the loving, gentle voice of God for yourself. So, now you hold in your hand years of the sweetest and most helpful times I personally have had. I began journaling down all the things God would speak to me long ago. I have supported each one with Scripture. I have learned not to listen just to reply, but to change. His Word never changes, but it will most definitely change our lives.

I challenge each of you to invest in spending time getting to know God, learn His nature and His character.

Just like you would get to know a best friend, find out all you can; share your heart and allow Him to share His

Develop such a constant awareness of Him that your ears are always listening for His voice.

In the pages ahead are the encouragements He has spoken to me. My prayer is that each one of them will speak to you as they have to me. And I encourage you to live with a pen and paper close by for all the times to come that He will gently tap you on the shoulder of your heart and say, "I've got something to tell you!" He is always revealing Himself to us. He calls you His friend and friends have a great time talking to each other.

Through my journaling, my own personal relationship with God has grown so intimate. I love knowing His presence and His voice, but most of all, I love Knowing Him.

My greatest desire for you is that you know Him and clearly hear His voice. Walk with me now in this wonderful interactive devotional of Hearing Love.

JOURNAL TITLES

15

How To Use This Journal

The margins are wide on each page for your interaction with what you hear.
Here are some suggestions:

- *Date the day the journal speaks to you and why;*

- *Underline what stands out;*

- *Write-out Scriptures in margins from the translation in your Bible;*

- *Write your own prayer at the bottom;*

- *Use colored pencils to doodle or color-code what stands out to you;*

- *Use blank pages in the back for your own notes.*

Enjoy reading over and over each entry. You will find different meanings will stand out each time.

God Bless You on your journey with *Hearing Love.*

~Char

I am safe in You!

Thank you for caring about what I care about... children, grands, health, my time, marriages, friends...

Safe With Me

There is a Calm in Me when your heart has been totally surrendered into My care. There is and will never be another who has the ability to care for you as I do. This world and all that is in it have nothing but self and all it's lust and pleasures as it's gods. Your heart is not safe in the cares of this life. So allow me, one situation at a time, to show you and prove to you that I am exactly who I say I am. I am trustworthy and faithful. I care for you and all that concerns you. Your heart and all that is in it is safe with Me. It is safe for you to love Me with all of your heart. For My love for you will never run out for all of eternity. I love you before time began, I love you now, I will love you forever.

I need to **Remember** this!!

I Cast all my cares upon Him! He Cares for Me 1 Peter 5:7

You are my **Rock!** Deu. 32:4

1 Peter 5:7   Deu. 32:4
Jer. 31:3

He loves me with an EVERLASTING LOVE He draws me with His loving Kindness

God, I ask for a full revelation of Your great love you have for me. I want to know You! You are SO GOOD!!

Let us rejoice and be glad and give Him glory!
REVELATION

29

Safe With Me

There is a calm in Me when your heart has been totally surrendered into My care. There is not, and will never be, another who has the ability to care for you as I do. This world, and all that is in it, have nothing but self with all its lusts and pleasures as its gods. Your heart is not safe in the cares of this life. So allow Me, one situation at a time, to show you and prove to you that I am exactly who I say I am. I am trustworthy and faithful. I care for you and all that concerns you. Your heart, and all that is in it, is safe with Me. It is safe for you to love Me with all of your heart. My love for you will never run out for all of eternity. I loved you before time began, I love you now, and I will love you forever.

1 Peter 5:7   Deuteronomy 32:4

Jeremiah 31:3

God, I ask for a full revelation of the great love You have for me. I want to know You. You are so good.

Lean Into Me

With a simple whisper you can give Me your day. Moment by moment, a simple lean into trusting Me can soothe your heart. Although it doesn't seem to be a simple thing to do, I assure you that your surrender will land securely in My arms. My arms are not so short that I cannot reach you. Your life, your days, your moments are filled with My loving guidance and light. Lean into My arms. Feel the rhythms of My steps. I know where we are going. I know the plans I have for you.

Proverbs 4:5   Isaiah 50:2

Jeremiah 29:11

Father, help me to always lean into You and trust You in all my ways.

Don't Trip and Fall

I am faithful to bring you times of refreshing and rebuilding. A coming of newness will spring forth just as a flower blooms. Focus on Me and My leading. I have your steps ordered. Your life has been paid for. Never doubt that your destiny awaits you. Give of yourself to Me. Keep your eyes focused on Me. Don't trip and fall over the things that take your mind off of Me. It is okay to expect great things, because I am great and I am in the things to come. You will find Me when you seek Me with all your heart.

Acts 3:19   Hebrews 12:2

Proverbs 8:17

Father, thank You for bringing refreshing to my life, that my steps are ordered by You and that Your eyes are always on me.

A Warm Blanket

Rest in Me. I delight to feel your soul surrender. Allow the songs I sing over you to deliver you from your fear. My perfect love, that is constant and sure, will cover you like a warm blanket. The warmth of My love casts out the cold doubts and fears. Fear is not your friend. Do not make a comfortable place in your mind for fear to live. Make no dwelling places for doubt. Should they knock and force their way in, give them no place to call home. Remind them of the songs of perfect love and deliverance that I am constantly singing over you.

Zephaniah 3:17   1 John 4:18

Ephesians 4:27

Father, thank you that Your perfect love casts out all my fears. Help me give no place to doubt and fear in my mind. Thank You for the songs of love that You sing over me.

Live In That Stream

Listen through the noise. Trust through the confusion. Never lose sight of Me. Set your face like flint toward Me. It may seem difficult to hear beyond the sounds of your own reasoning at times, but My voice is greater still. Your eyes may be tempted to wander to the things of this world where sin so easily entangles your soul, but in setting your focus on Me comes the healing salve of grace to comb through the tangled messes we make. Freedom waits for grace to do its work and then grace gives way to joy. Joy is the stream that flows from My presence. Live in that stream.

Hebrews 12:1   Psalm16:11

Isaiah 50:7

Father, thank You that Your voice is louder than the noise I hear from this world. I choose to place my focus on You and live in the stream of Your presence.

See What I See

Hold back your judgment. Be slow to speak. See what I see. See with your heart. Feel with My compassion before your tongue runs free with harmful words. Grace has been given to you. You have freely received, now you must freely give. Take notice of the lonely. I will point them out to you. Speak kindness to the broken hearted. Many are searching for Me and I will show Myself to them through you. Follow Me. I will make you "fishers of men." Follow Me. Learn of Me. I will show you My ways.

James 1:19   *Matthew5:19*

Matthew 20:39

Father, help me hold my tongue from harmful words. Help me see with compassion. Teach me Your ways.

Today's Mercy and Grace

Do not worry about tomorrow. I know you think you know what tomorrow's problems are going to be, but I have only supplied you the grace for today. Today My mercy was new for you. Mercy for what today holds. But I did not supply the mercy and grace for tomorrow. When you wake tomorrow that mercy will be yours. Please, child, do not attempt to face tomorrow's problems with today's mercy and grace. Trust that I will always supply what you need when you need it. Not only does tomorrow have its own problems, it also has its own mercy and its own sustaining grace.

Matthew 6:25-34

Lamentations 3:22-23

Father, thank You that for each new day I always have the mercy and grace that I need. Teach me to walk in mercy and grace.

Peace To Your Storms

Let My peace umpire in your mind today. Your own thoughts and expectations will hold you captive. Be willing to release your disappointments to Me and allow Me to bring peace to your storms. When you forget that My peace is here for you, the storms seem more fierce; but when My peace is already present the storms become small rain showers that can ultimately produce growth. My purpose for dying was to leave peace for you to walk in. Don't leave peace on the sidelines to only call on when you feel your need for it. Walk in it every moment of every day. It is My gift to you.

Colossians 3:15   Philippians4:7

John 14:27

Father, thank You for the gift of Your peace. I choose to walk in Your peace today.

Make Yourself At Home

I offer compassion to you this day. I know the thoughts of your heart. I can hear the cries of your spirit. I am interceding to My Father for you. I never slumber or sleep. I do not grow weary or tired. I do not neglect to give you every good and perfect gift. In My presence you will find fullness of joy, and in My right hand I have pleasures that will last forever. Dwell here with Me. Stay in My presence. Make yourself at home abiding with Me.

Romans 8:3-35   Psalms16:11

James 1:17

Father, I trust everything about You and I receive all that You are. I choose to make myself at home in You today.

In Plain View

Goodness is all around you, for I am good. Notice Me in the small things that are easily overlooked. Count the blessings I have bathed your life in. Train your eyes to recognize goodness as I see goodness. Do not use the definition that this world has given to define for you what My goodness is. Seek My heart and learn of Me. When you do this with all of your heart, you will find Me. I am not hiding. I am in plain view, always. Look for Me. Find Me. I am in the goodness.

Psalm 34:8   Jeremiah 29:13

Psalm 100:5

Help me to recognize goodness as You see it. I know You are all around me. I choose today to be sensitive to Your leading. Teach me to hear You clearly.

Listen For My Voice

Listen for My voice. Listen for Me saying, "This is the way, walk in it". I am standing beside you to keep you from wandering. I am in front of you leading the way. I am a light that shines in the darkness. I am behind you lest you fall. I sing over you with songs of deliverance. I am all around you, child. Listen, I am leading you. Follow Me, and together we will change the world.

Isaiah 30:21   Psalm 119:105

Psalm 32:7

Father, I am so thankful that You are all around me. I choose today to be sensitive to Your leading. Teach me to hear You clearly

Remember

If today should seem hard for you, remember: nothing is too hard for Me. Should the task in front of you seem impossible, remember: nothing is impossible for Me. If you cannot understand and your mind is confused, remember: I bring wisdom and understanding to those who ask. Cast your cares into the waters of My love. Let go of the burdens you so eagerly attempt to hold onto and carry. Trust with all your heart I am here with you and I will never leave.

Jeremiah 32:27 Luke 1:37

1 Peter 5:7

Father, I choose to let go of all the things I hold on to today. I release them into the waters of Your love. Thank You for caring so deeply for me.

Shift Your World

I have put a song in your heart, and a new song in your mouth. Sounds of praise to fill the air, and melodies of love for My ears to hear! And as you sing to Me, I will sing over you. The atmosphere around you will change into one of joy and delight; worship and adoration. I long to hear your voice speaking and singing My word and My songs. Shift your world with the sounds of My spirit flowing out of the deep well inside of you. This is My day, rejoice, sing and be glad in it.

Psalm 40:3   Psalm 118:24

Psalm 98:1

Father, today I will choose to let the songs in my heart shift the atmosphere around me. I will let my praise rise to Your ears. Thank You for this day and for the power of worship.

The Gift

Every good and perfect gift comes from Me. My gifts have the touch of heaven in them. The touch from a baby's hand, the smile from a friend, a kind word from a stranger: gifts that bring you life and peace. The awe of the ocean, the majesty of a snow capped mountain: gifts that cause you to worship. Warm sunshine and a soft, soaking rain: gifts that cause you to grow. Forgiveness, redeeming love, grace, mercy and truth, the cross, the empty tomb: gifts that give abundant life. I will freely give you all things because the gifts are in Me… I am the Gift.

James 1:17   John 3:16

Romans 8:32

Father, thank You. There is none like You.

Lovesick Lover

I am mindful of you. Like a lovesick lover, My thoughts are on you. You are the apple of My eye. I see your heart and know your intricate parts. I formed you in secret and planned your days, I gave gentle thoughts to your destiny. I shine a bright light on your path every moment. Never wonder if I am with you. I promise to never leave you. I am yours and you are Mine. Walk out today with great joy in My presence, sure of My unfailing love for you.

Proverbs 7:2   Psalms139:15

Psalm 119:105   Deuteronomy 31:6

Thank You for loving me, Lord. I know You are with me; You make me feel so loved.

The Way Maker

When you look around and you can't find your way, remember I am the way maker. I make ways where there seems to be no way; when your paths look crooked and confused, when the wind seems to toss you back and forth. Remember, I am the one who can make crooked paths straight, and by a word, I can calm the wind. When worry crowds your mind and doubt bombards your heart, remember that I ask you to let Me carry those and you carry My peace. Live in trust and rest in Me. My yoke is easy.

Isaiah 43:16 Isaiah 45:2

Luke 3:5   Matthew 11:30

Father, I choose to trust You to light my path. I trust You to make all of the crooked places straight for me. Light my way with Your word.

Hidden In My Strength

My strength is made perfect in your weakness child. When weakness comes and tries to slow you down, I am with you in perfect strength. You see, perfect strength is when you fall into Me and allow Me to hide you. When you are hidden in My strength, your weakness can't be seen. The only thing seen is Me and your complete dependency on Me to be strong for you. My perfect love casts out fear. My perfect strength carries you in weakness. So when you feel weak in your mind, your soul or your body, know that I am with you to give you My perfect strength and help you overcome anything. Nothing is impossible with Me.

2 Corinthians 12:9   1 John 4:18

Hide me in Your strength today, Father. You carry me in my weaknesses and cause me to be brave and have courage. I know I can do all things through the one of gives me strength.

Once Again

Your false expectations of the way you think things should be will always crowd Me out. When your mind is full of selfish ways it is hard for you to hear My voice. Oh, that your trust would be in My never-failing love for you. I long for your surrender to My ways. This world will draw you into selfishness and hold you captive. You self-destruct in the place where you strive to be right. Surrender of the will is denying your rights to My ways. Over and over I ask for your trust. So once again child, I ask… trust Me.

Proverbs 3:5-6   Psalms 25:4

Psalm 86:11

Father, I do want to trust You with all of my heart. I do confess that my selfishness gets in my way. Once again, I surrender to You and Your ways in my life.

Come Sit A While

If your soul feels wounded and disappointment crowds your mind, come away with Me. My heart bids you to come sit a while with me. Let me remind you whose you are. Allow Me to tell you again of My great love for you. This world will convince you that you have no worth. The voices in your past will tell you there is no future. Let Me, your shepherd, speak to you because you are Mine and you know My voice. Be careful not to listen to another voice. Not one from your past, nor one from the enemy. My words are life to you. Choose life.

Jeremiah 31:3   John10:27

Deuteronomy 30:19

Father, when I am down, I choose to turn my ear to You. All my hope is in You. My life is in You only.

The Gardener

Gentle rains of My grace are falling down all around you; the evidence that I am near you. Just as rain soaks the ground and the seeds that lie dormant, I water the seeds in you. I am the gardener and the vinedresser. I have planted seeds in you that have not yet broken the ground to reach the light. I am sending the rain of My spirit to bring forth the roots and cause the gifts to grow to full maturity. You will bring forth fruit for Me that I will use to nurture and feed others with. The growth in you will cause growth in others. Do not hide My gifts or bury them. Use them for My glory and My purposes. I will cause the harvest!

John 15

Father, please help me always to be good ground for the seeds You plant in me. Call forth the fruit in me to nurture others. I choose to bring glory to You through the harvest of my life. You are my gardener.

<u>Trustworthy</u>

When you do not know what to do, look to Me. I am the one who can fight your battles for you. Put all of your confidence in Me. Place your feet firmly on the foundations of My word. None of man's ideas and ways will help when you need Me most. Steal away with Me and talk to me. I will answer you. Place all your faith in Me because I am the one who is the author and the finisher of your very faith. Your faith is within Me. You can place it in My hands. Once you place your faith in My hands, trust Me. I am trustworthy. Rest securely and dwell safely in My presence.

Psalm 20:7   Isaiah 28:16

Psalm 3:4

Father, I choose to place my faith in You. When I don't know what to do, I know that I can trust You. You are my trustworthy God. I know that I can rest securely and dwell safely in Your presence always. Have overcome this world and your destiny is in Me.

Carrier Of All I Am

My spirit is with you, in you! You are the very carrier of all I am. It is through you the world will know Me. This is no small thing. The days are ahead that others will search for Me and find Me when they find you. I will send them. They will surely come. Stay close to Me. Seek Me with all your heart. For I have planted in you a garden that is growing for a time of harvest. Others will come to eat of the fruit and be nourished. Feed My sheep. Give them bread from heaven, the very words from My mouth. Be not timid. Hold back nothing. Harvest time comes quickly.

Ezekiel 37:27 John 13:35

Father, I long to be that place of nourishment for others, a safe place for others to find You. I choose not to hold back or be timid. I will set my heart toward the harvest and reap them for You.

Swap With Me

When the weight of this world lays heavy on you and your head is hard to lift, shift your focus to Me. My yoke is easy and My burden is light. Allow your heavy feeling to signal you that you have taken too much on yourself. Troubles come, but I have overcome this world. Swap with Me. You give Me your cares, and I will give you My peace. You don't ever have to face anything alone. When I said I would never leave you, it was a promise. You can rest in Me knowing that I am working all things together for good. Set your focus on Me. Trust Me at all times, with all situations, and let Me be the glory and the lifter of your head.

Matthew 11:28-30 Romans8:28

Psalm 3:3

Father, I choose to swap with You. My cares do get heavy. Thank you for Your peace. My eyes are on You.

Let Me Tell You

Come away with Me and let Me tell you of My love. I am always mindful of you. My love for you is deeper than the deepest ocean. My love stretches wider than time and space. My love for you is higher than the heavens above you. My love for you will never stop, it will last forever. My love endures through anything and everything. It is My pleasure and joy to give you every good and perfect gift. I sing songs of love over you and dance all around you. Not only is it true that I will never leave you, I never want to leave you. I am yours, and you are Mine.

Ephesians 3:17-18   _Psalm 136_

Zephaniah 3:17

Father, help me understand the depths of Your love for me. I open my hands to receive the vastness of all I don't understand.

I Am Easily Found

Quiet yourself child. Your searching has turned to striving. My yoke is easy and I am easily found by you. Don't look so hard for the experience of My presence that you run right past Me. For in itself My presence is enough. In all you have done, rest. Reflect in gratitude for the life I have given you. In all you will do, rest. Look forward in gratitude that every day unfolds My plan and purposes for you. Purpose in your heart to seek Me and to listen for My voice. Be fully awake to My spirit and watch and see what I will do.

Matthew 11:28-30   Jeremiah 29:12-14

Father, I choose to rest in gratitude today. I know my striving can get in the way of me seeing You clearly. I want to be fully awake and watching for You in every area of my life.

Peace Train

My goal today is to keep you in perfect peace. Your goal must be to keep your mind on Me and to trust Me. I know your anxious thoughts and the way your mind can get so crowded and confused. My remedy for that is that you keep your thoughts toward Me. Remember the ways I have led you and guided you. Think on the ways I have made for you when there seemed to be none. There is no one like Me, for I am your peace. It's not peace like the world gives, it comes through My spirit. It passes your understanding like a fast moving train. Trust Me today and live in My perfect peace.

Isaiah 26:3   John 14:27

Father, today I choose to trust You and keep my mind on You. You have given me peace over and over again. There is truly no one like You. Thank you for Your unfailing peace in my life.

Forever Reaching You

Rejoice today; For My love is drawing you with everlasting love. My great kindness is forever reaching you. Don't pull away from the promptings of My love. I desire to continually bless you over and over again. To take your hand in Mine and walk with you just as I did with Adam and Eve. I long to talk with you and share My heart and tell you things to come. I call you friend. Spending time with you is what I created you for. I long for you to have fullness of joy. When you are with Me, that joy is all around us. Together, we experience that joy. I draw you into Me with My everlasting love and kindness.

Jeremiah 31:3   John 15:15

John 16:13

Thank You, Lord, that You never stop reaching for me. Thank You that You show Your friendship to Me and desire my friendship with You. Your joy is my delight. Continue to draw me.

Allow Me

Even in this fallen world I have set around you the ways I love you. I continually give gifts and attempt to 'woo' you to Myself. My goodness and My gifts are given so you will love Me. My jealousy is great and I long for your affection. I have crowned your head with My faithful love. I promise to never leave you or be unfaithful to you. I offer you all that I am to be yours. Love not this world more than Me. I loved you first and desire your love in return. Allow Me to show you My love, it's all around you. I long to meet every desire within your heart.

James 1:17   Hebrews13:5

1 John 4:19

Today, I choose to see Your love for me, Lord. You are so kind and faithful to me. Thank You for Your amazing love.

Beginning To End

When morning breaks into song and another day for you begins, reach for Me and I will take hold of your hand. I have already seen this day from beginning to end. I can guide you through each step. My way may not be your way, but I can promise you that it will be the best one for you. All I ask of you is to yield. Yield into Me and I will direct you with My eye on you. I will not leave you to guess. I will reveal Myself and My ways. Take time to slow down and listen. This day can be one to rejoice in. When night calls to reflect, you will look back and see Me.

Isaiah 55:9   Psalm 118:24

Father, each day is such an amazing gift from You. Reveal Yourself to me as I slow down and listen to You. Make me aware of Your presence every moment.

Refreshing Presence

Today, I will blow winds of refreshing your way. Just as on a hot and dry day you long for a cool breeze and a drink of water, so I Am. I can quench every thirst of your soul and cause the wind of My Holy Spirit to blow over you. If you ever feel the need for refreshing and renewing of your strength, I am here. My words will feed you and restore life to you. I am like a stream in the desert places. I never meant for you to dwell in the dry, desert places. I long to lead you to green pastures and still waters. Dwell in My refreshing presence and rest.

Isaiah 41:18   Psalm 23:2

Acts 3:19 b

I long to dwell in Your refreshment, Father. Thank You that You quench all of my thirst and continually feed my soul with Your word. Today I choose to dwell in You.

Moving Ahead

I do not desire you to walk forward while looking backwards. Many things from the past can hold you captive and imprison you. Trying to move forward with your eyes focused on what is behind you will cause you to veer off track. Your feet will stumble and cause you to fall. It is My desire for you to remember the past and what it has taught you, but not allow yourself to fixate your eyes on it. Set your eyes on Me. Let the light I have placed on your path illuminate the way for you. I don't want your feet to become entangled in sins that will trip you and cause you to lose your stability. Remember the past, but focus on moving ahead with Me.

Philippians 3:13   Hebrews 12:1-2

Lord, help me to not walk forward looking backward at my past. I want to fix my eyes on You and move with You. You have my future in Your hands, so I will hold tight to You.

Seed Planting

Plant seeds of kindness today along your way. Seed planting is the basic way of My kingdom growing around you. The seeds of weeds are being thrown out in this world that will try to choke the seeds of My fruit. The fruit of My Spirit has the life you want in it, so to have it, you must plant it. Sow deep into the hearts of others. Let the water of My words be in your mouth and the light of My presence shine from your life, so that everywhere you go, you can be planting and giving life to all the seeds of My kingdom that are sown. Some plant, some water, some harvest. You can do all three!

1 Corinthians 3:6-8

Father, help me to be mindful that along my way, I am always planting seeds into someone's life. I pray I can water and harvest what has already been planted by others. Keep me aware and alert, and help me to feel Your nudges in my spirit.

People Need Me
People Need You

Don't get in a hurry. Don't allow yourself to rush your way through this one life I have given you. My purposes are all about people. My kingdom is about people. If you are too preoccupied with time, places, and things, you will miss multiple opportunities to touch a life that I place in your path. Things don't need Me, deadlines don't need Me, schedules don't need Me… people need Me. I am in you, so that means people need you. I will direct you to whom, when and where. I will give you My compassion and My thoughts. I will even give you the words to say. Allow Me to slow you down and show Myself to others through you.

2 Corinthians 3:2-3   Matthew 5:14-16

Father, help me to always remember that Your kingdom is all about people. I don't ever want to be so busy that I miss these moments You give me with someone. Slow me down from my agenda and show me Yours.

A Way Out

I will always make a way of escape to you child. When you feel trapped by the enemy or you sense him setting up an ambush against you, keep your eyes looking for Me. I will provide a way of escape. Nothing the enemy entangles you with is too hard for Me to deliver you out of. It may seem that the subtle ways and craftiness of his tactics are strong and have the ability to hold you forever, but that is a lie. I will always provide you a way out and shine a light that will lead you to wholeness. Shake off the chains that bind you and run toward Me. I am always with you.

1 Corinthians 10:13

Father, thank You for always providing me with a way of escape. When I am trapped, open my eyes to see You and Your ways. Show me Your ways that I may walk in them all the days of my life.

Our Love Songs

I not only sing over you, but I have put a song of praise in your mouth. Even though no one else even hears it, I have given you a song. Let your mouth sing praises to Me. Music is powerful warfare against the enemy. Our love songs to each other cannot be comprehended by the enemies that stand against you. Darkness does not comprehend love. So, when our love is being expressed in song to one another the enemy is in total confusion. As I sing over you, and you in return sing your song back to Me, we create a continuous chorus of love between us that no one can stand against.

2 Chronicles 20:20-23

I choose to not only listen to Your song over me, but to respond with songs of love and praise back to You. Thank You for Your love for me. I love the intimate ways You choose to show me Your love. Thank You for the powerful strength of our songs.

<u>Never Ending Supply</u>

I delight in showering you with grace. Even though My grace is undeserved, it never runs out. I never tire of pouring out My gifts of grace in abundance to you. This never ending supply of gifts of grace show My never ending and unfailing love I have for you. I also delight in sharing My truth with you. To see you receive the revelation of My truth about who I am and how I see you and to watch you receive the freedom that brings you is My delight. Because I know that when My gift of grace kisses the truth of My word in you, you will walk in My perfect love and freedom. In other words, you will walk with Me.

Jeremiah 31:3   Ephesians 2:4-5

Psalm 85:10

Thank You for pouring out Your grace on me. I am so blessed to stand under Your fountain that never runs dry. I desire to be full of Your truth. I want Your truth and grace to kiss and my life and cause Your freedom to be mine. My heart's desire is to walk with You.

Steady, Sure and Solid

I am a steady and sure place for you. I am a solid rock for you to stand on. I am not hollow or fragile. You can trust that when you plant your feet on Me, that I cannot be shaken. I do not crumble under pressure. I am a sure foundation for your life. I am not a pile of loose gravel that can shift and change with every quake or step. I am a solid and smooth surface so that your stance can be stable and strong. You can't wage war if the ground beneath you won't hold you up. I not only make your feet like hinds feet, I am the solid rock and cornerstone for you to stand strong on. You can trust in Me.

Psalm 40:2-4   Habakkuk 3:19

God, You are my rock. I plant my feet securely in You. I desire to be stable and steady as Your disciple. Thank You that You cause my feet not to stumble. Help me to walk securely before You and others.

I Fight For You

When you walk hand in hand with Me, I become a shield around you. I protect you from the dangers that you never see with your eyes, the arrows that fly by day and night in the spirit to harm you and bring destruction. I cover you and shield you. As you lean into Me and allow My blood to cover you and walk in My footsteps, you begin to look like Me; And the shield of My glory and presence covers you. Trust Me to be your shield. Know that I fight for you. You are never alone to battle for yourself. I am your shield and your defender, your glory and the lifter of your head!

Psalm 91:1-2,5   Psalm 3:3

Help me, Father, to see that You are a shield around me. You fight for me even when I cannot see. I trust You completely to cover me and be my defender. Thank You for never leaving me alone.

<u>You Will Find Me</u>

With all of your heart, seek My wisdom. I have not placed you here to live and try to figure things out on your own. I have been made for you wisdom. I have provided what you need to learn how to live. I have given you instruction and truths for you to walk in. I did not leave you helpless; I provided the Holy Spirit and My Word to teach you. The listening, learning and applying is your part. Seek Me while I may be found. Learn of Me. I came to give you abundant life. Walk in wisdom and understanding for you will find Me when you seek Me with all your heart.

1 Corinthians 1:30   Jeremiah 29:13

Jesus, I know that You have given me wisdom. Give me eyes to see and ears to hear Your voice. I long to apply Your word in every area of my life. Teach me Your ways.

I Was There

When you could not see Me, I was there. When you could not feel Me, My hand was on you. When you could not hear Me, I was continuously singing over you. When you blamed me for what happened, My eyes cried with unconditional love for you. You see child, I made a promise to never leave you or forsake you. No matter the circumstances of this fallen world, no matter how far it pushes Me out, I will remain true to My word and I will not leave you. I have placed eternity in your heart with My purposes in mind, and together, we will fulfill the perfect plan for you. Trust Me and My love for you.

Hebrews 13:5 Ecclesiastes 3:11

Thank You for always being with me, even when I am unaware. I know Your plan for me is perfect. I choose to trust You today in every circumstance. I know You will faithfully guide me. I love You.

Let's Go Fishing

Let's go fishing for men today. I know you get weary when you haven't had a catch in a while, but I can show you where to cast your net. I know the places where you can find the largest catch of the day. But first, you have to let Me in your boat, in your life. In order to fish, we will need bait; and I have chosen to make you the bait. So let me in your boat to teach you how to be the bait that will attract others to Me, and together, we can draw them into your boat so you can help them become the bait for others. This is my way of making you a disciple, a fisher of men.

Matthew 4:19 Mark 1:17

Father, help me to be the one that attracts others to You. Just as the fish are drawn to bait, I want to be what makes others come to You. Make me a true disciple; teach me what that is as I follow You.

Just Be With Me

Come away with Me today for a while. Sit with Me beside a still water river bank that flows with My peace. Breathe in the refreshing fragrance of My presence. There need not be words exchanged while we abide here together. Just be still and know that I am your God. Allow assurance to wash away any doubts. Trust My perfect love to cause all fear to leave. Just BE with Me; leave all else. Dip your heart into the calmness of My love. Stay as long as you can, come as often as you want, I am always here waiting.

Mark 6:31-33   Song of Solomon 2:10

I love being with You, Lord. I choose to come often to this place where we can be together. You are my peace. I breathe You in. I love my moments with You.

Even Then

I call you to remembrance this day that it was I who made you. I knit you in your mother's womb. I heard your first heartbeat. Even then, I knew the plans I have for you. Even then, eternity was placed in you with purpose. I have guided you with My eye on you and will continue to guide you. I hold on to you with my right hand. You have never been without My love and you never will. Keep in step with me and move to the rhythms of My grace. There you will know the flow of My Spirit and the 'wooing' of My voice. You are Mine and your ears are tuned to hear and know Me. Just as I heard your first heartbeat, now listen for Mine.

Psalm 139:13-16   Isaiah 41:10

I choose today to remember that it is You who formed me. It is You who guides me and holds me together. I choose to listen for Your voice to guide me. Thank You for loving me and calling me Your own. I love You.

Taste and See

I long to satisfy your soul with good things; I am the bread of life. Every word of Mine is meat for your bones. Living water flows from Me with life-giving power. My forgiveness flowing in you will detox the poisons that can destroy you. I provide joy and gladness to medicate your pain. My peace is always available to quiet your stress. My love can and will drive out every fear. Give thanks and take and eat of the goodness I give. Taste and see that I am good. Hunger and thirst for Me, for only I can truly satisfy your soul.

Psalm 34:8   Psalm63:1-5

Psalm 107:8-9

Lord, You are so good to me. You are the only one who satisfies. You are bread, meat, and water for my soul. You are my gladness, my peace, and my joy. I am complete in You!

Leave It Here

I want you to cast your cares and worries on Me today. I have great compassion and care for the things that concern you. My ears have heard your cries even in the late night hours. In the secret times when your heart unloads its burdens, I am there. You can make no changes in any situation by worrying. Nothing is accomplished by the fretting of your heart. But if you will place everything in My hands, I can change and mend. I can redeem and make all of it work together for good. My hands are open and ready to receive. Leave it here. Trust Me to do what only I can do, and walk in My peace.

1 Peter 5:7   Matthew 11:28

Father, help me remember I can make no changes by worrying. I choose to place everything in Your well able hands and rest in Your abiding peace.

Admire The Landscape

When it seems like life has set a mountain before you to climb, I will be with you providing every place for your foot to step. When you see a valley in front of you that seems too deep to walk through, I will be here to carry you through. Nothing is too hard for Me, even if your heart and your flesh feel it is. My strength will lift you up to the place where you can look back and admire the landscape you have crossed over. The journey is to be taken with Me. Abide in Me as we walk together. I am always here.

Psalm 121:3   Jeremiah 33:27

Psalm 91:1

Father, sometimes it feels too hard, but I know I can trust You. And as I abide in you, I will be able to look back and know that You have seen me through.

<u>Angels</u>

I have given you a gift, a guardian angel to watch over you in all your ways. I have provided ministering, warring angels to fight for you and do your bidding. These are my gifts to you. They will help protect you. They have swords drawn to fight over you in the spirit. They wait and listen for your voice to commission them. They are sent to you and for you. Know that the spirit world fights for your life. Pray in My spirit and set your ministering angels in motion. They await your command.

Hebrews 1:14 Daniel 10:13

Psalm 91:11

Thank You Lord for the gifts of Angels. I receive their ministry to me and for me. Thank You for caring for me in such an amazing way.

Unbound By Chains

I came to break the chains that have you bound, child. I came to unlock the old and the new chains that you have allowed to tangle around your feet. I came to break the chain, but you must unwrap it and throw it off. You are the one who must lay it aside. Walk away from the snares that attempt to hold on to you, and keep you from Me. I have unlocked the locks and broken the chains, so that you no longer have to be a prisoner. Walk in My freedom. Unbound by chains, you will move freely in Me.

Isaiah 61:1   Hebrews12:1

John 8:36

Jesus, I know You came to set the captives free. I choose to lay aside the chains that You have unlocked and broken. I choose to walk in freedom with You.

Eyes Wide Open

Enter into My presence with thanksgiving today. Slow down and be aware of all the goodness I have given to you. The gifts will just keep coming every day. I long to load you down with blessings, I long for you to overflow with My offerings to you. I already do this every day, but you are too busy to see. You walk right past amazing graces that I set before you. Stop and look around you. Be still and listen. With eyes wide open you will begin to thank Me and find yourself in My presence with fullness of joy.

Psalm 100:4   Psalm 46:10

Psalm 68:19

Thank You for Your amazing love for me. Tune my heart to Your heartbeat so I can recognize all You do. I don't want to miss anything from You.

Always Available

My presence is like a refreshing, cool breeze on a hot day. When life has left you parched and dry, I will bring a soaking rain of My spirit to revive you. When your thirst is desperate to be satisfied, I am the only water that can satisfy. You see child, it is not My desire for you to ever be caught in a desert place, because My endless, bountiful supply for you will never run out. Water for your soul and food for your spirit are always available. You need not wander in desert places. Come to the table I have set out before you. Refresh yourself with Me.

Isaiah 43:19   John 4:14   John 6:35

Father, truly You alone can satisfy my soul.

Open Hands

Come before Me with open hands. If I try to give you gifts and your hands are closed, receiving is impossible. When your fist shakes in anger and bitterness and your heart closes tight, there is no place to lay My blessings down. Don't let anyone or anything cause you to clinch your fist and keep you from My blessings. Forgive, as I have forgiven you. Walk free of offenses, lay down all your pride. Know that the life I have for you is peace and rest, with My joy flowing freely in you. Open your hands to Me. Reach and receive My gifts. You will overflow with blessings.

Psalm 119:165   Matthew 6:14

I choose today to forgive any offenses. I choose to forgive any wrongs done to me. I want to walk in your peace all the days of my life.

I Call You Friend

Take time to listen to Me. I really can reveal to you the things you long to know. I can teach you by My spirit and show you things to come. I will prepare you for the days ahead and manifest My plan for you. My voice is not a mystery to you. I call you friend. When you receive Me and know Me as friend, My voice will be easy to recognize. I am not a stranger with strange ways you can't understand. I am a friend who loves you, wants to talk with you and spend time with you. Listen with ears to hear what My spirit is saying and you will hear Me clearly.

John 15:15   John 10:27

Jeremiah 33:3

I love my friendship with You, Lord. Your faithfulness to speak to me is my delight. I love being with You.

I Will Be A Shelter

Troubles and trials will come and go in this life, but I will not leave you alone. The pressures of daily living and the concerns for tomorrow crowd in on your mind. They cause confusion but I will never leave you alone. Lean into Me during these times when you feel weary. Draw from My strength when you feel yours is gone. I will be your shelter from every storm. And I can take every circumstance and make it work together for good. Rest your mind from trying to figure out details and trust Me to show you each step. You are sheltered in My love and under My shadow you can safely abide.

John 16:33   Proverbs 3:5-7

Psalm 91:1

I choose today to rest in You, Lord. Thank You that I can abide in Your shelter. I am so secure in You.

The Key of Kindness

I give My kindness to draw and lead people to a place of repentance, so today I ask you to do the same. Give kindness to the ones that you think will never bend. Share a caring word with someone who feels distant and far away. Do something nice for someone who you feel does not deserve it. Wrapped up in kindness is My love. My love has the power to draw people to Me. Let kindness be seen and heard from you today and watch My power at work in the hearts of everyone you meet. It is a key in My kingdom that unlocks and opens doors that no man can shut.

Romans 2:4   Ephesians 4:32

John 13:35

Thank You for all the kindness you have shown to me, Lord. Help me today to show kindness in all I do to everyone I see. Help me to show Your love.

Blessed You Will Be

I have given you all you need in My word. My words are not just pretty words for you to quote so that you can sound wise to others. My words are life to you. They bring health to your bones. I desire you to live by every word I have spoken. I don't allow My words to pass away because they are your source in this life. The wisdom of man will leave you empty and searching, but My words will give understanding even to the simple. Hide My word in your heart. Meditate day and night on My ways. Learn of Me and allow Me to teach you. For blessed you will be when you choose to walk in My word.

Proverbs 4:22 Joshua 1:8

Your word is light and life to me, Lord. I choose today to hide Your word in my heart and meditate on it day and night. Your word sustains my life.

New Days Ahead

Enjoy the freshness of this new day. Take a deep breath and forget the past and press forward. There is much behind you that doesn't need your attention anymore. All has been washed and covered in My blood. There is much ahead that is worth reaching for. So stretch your arms out to Me and dive into new vision for your life. Don't settle and remain stuck where you are. There are many opportunities waiting on only you. New days ahead are inviting you to rejoice in the fact that you are not done yet. I still have much for you. Reach for it, don't wait on it. Pursue what's in front of you and forget what lies behind.

Philippians 3:13-14

Lord, I choose today to leave behind the past and reach and press into today. I desire to move forward with You in Your goodness. Help me keep my eyes on You.

The Path Ahead

Never forget that I go before you. I know what you need before you ever ask me. There truly is a light that shines on the path ahead of you. Your steps are made in faith toward total trust in Me. You need to never wander aimlessly in this life. Darkness cannot overtake the light I have provided for every step. When the prince of darkness tempts you into his dark places, turn around and walk toward My light. If there is no light on your path, search your ways; Examine your steps. Call to Me and My voice will guide you back to the light and all the way home to Me.

Matthew 6:8   Psalm 119:105

Isaiah 30:21

Thank You, Lord, for the light you give me to walk in. I don't ever want to stay off of Your path and way for me. Hold on tight so I won't fail.

Perfect Union

Remember all My benefits. I have given you everything you need to live an amazing abundant life. Place no heavy value on the things that pass away. Do not give your affections to things that cannot satisfy your soul. I long to be in perfect union with you so that every blessing and promise I have offered to you is in plain view for you to receive. My gifts can get covered up in the shadows of worldly things that have no worth. Be careful that what delights you is in Me. For what delights Me is in you. If you will delight yourself in Me I will give you the desires of your heart.

Psalm 103:2   Psalm 37:4

Thank You for all the benefits You love to give me. I choose to delight myself in You and not in the things of this world. You are so good to me.

Never Rush Away

Don't miss My smiles. There are times that My pleasure overwhelms and causes a smile from heaven to break out all around you. You will sense these times because they carry the weight of My glory with them; a blanket of heavy glory that pleasures the soul. When you know these times and recognize them, stay and allow My glory to bathe you in My pleasure. Soak yourself through and through so that nothing is left untouched by My grace. Great strength is found in these moments and you will carry it with you. My glory will lift you and cover you on your way. When My glory smiles on you, abide there. Never rush away.

Song of Solomon 2:10

Psalm 3:3

Shower me with Your glory God. I want to see and recognize all You are doing around me today. I need Your strength and covering. I choose to abide in You.

Listen To My Wisdom

I have freely offered My wisdom to you. You never need to wonder about what to do. Ask Me. If you lack wisdom in any situation, I have promised to help you. Many fret and worry about what to do and where to go; they waste time that could be given to seeking and hearing My plans and directions. Don't ask anyone else before you talk to Me. I can tell you even who can help you. Wrong guidance will cripple and delay. Bad advice will stop your progress. Give your ear to listen to My wisdom; I have promised it to you if you ask Me. I give it freely and will never guide you wrong. I care very deeply for you.

James 1:5   Matthew 6:25

Thank You for Your promise of wisdom for me. I know You care for me and want to guide me. I am asking for Your wisdom in every area of my life. I choose to follow You.

Enjoy Your Days With Me

Time ticks by. Minutes and hours slip into days and weeks. I do not desire your life to be filled with regrets of wasted days. With each new day, each new moment, I present to you new opportunities to see Me and My love for you. My love notes to you are everywhere. Never forget that I designed you so that I could have you as My friend. I never get weary in watching you, I always long to hear your voice. I watch for your eyes to turn their gaze toward Me. I long for your stillness so I can touch you and you will know it's My hand. I delight in giving you gifts, promises and blessings. Enjoy your days with Me. Let Me love you through all your days, all the way home to Me.

Jeremiah 31:3 Psalm 136:4

Your great love amazes me. I don't want to waste any of my days, Lord. I choose to let you love me. I receive Your great love, both now and forever.

I Am So Jealous

My love for you is not fickle. I will never love you today but not tomorrow. I give to you an everlasting love. Sure and steady. All I ask is that you love Me with all your heart. Many love Me only if I meet their expectations. Many only say they give Me their hearts if and when I will rescue and heal. Many love others and other things more than they love Me. I am so jealous. I want your love so desperately. I have given even the life of My son. I have written My love in the sky and in all of creation. I want your love and affection to be toward Me. I promise to love you with an unconditional, eternal love that will never leave you wanting for more. Do you love Me?

Deuteronomy 10:12   Luke10:27

Jeremiah 31:3

Thank You for loving me with a sure and steady love that never runs out. You never leave me wanting. You are my all in all. I love You, Lord.

Training and Taming

Humble yourself. Self requires an intense time of training and taming. Like a wild beast, self has a powerful prideful will. When your self is full of pride, there has to be a pouring out; a humbling, a spilling out. There is a horrible odor to pride that is usually not detected by the one it is in. It hurts and chases away most everyone it touches. But if you will humble yourself before Me, I will cause the stench of your pride to turn into a beautiful aroma of fragrant servanthood. Humbly serving others kills the effects of pride and causes it to die. I resist pride and give grace to humility. Serve with gladness knowing that I will never resist you but pour My grace out freely upon you.

James 4:6   1 Peter 5:5

Galatians 5:13

God, I don't want to be full of pride and You resist me. Teach me to serve with a humble heart. I want my life to be a sweet fragrance to You.

Kingdom Of Perfect Peace

I have promised a place of perfect peace for you. This place is never far from you. When you decide to keep your mind on Me and think of Me I will actually keep you in this place of peace. This world does not house places of such peace as I can give you. You can have moments of relief from worry and stress here in this world, but quickly the enemy will bombard your mind again. I can actually lock you in a place with Me of perfect peace when you choose to allow your thoughts to dwell on Me. You see I am the Prince of Peace, Ruler in the Kingdom of Perfect Peace. Abide here with Me and rest your mind.

John 14:27   Isaiah 9:6   Isaiah 26:3

Jesus, You are my Prince of Peace. I know when my eyes and my thoughts are on You I live in peace. Thank You for providing peace that passes my understanding.

Overwhelmed

Being overwhelmed with the cares of this world has never, and will never be part of My desire for you. The only thing I want you to be overwhelmed with is Me. My goodness and kindness is more than you can ever wrap your mind around. When you allow yourself to be overwhelmed by My very presence, and the truth of who I am envelops you in My grace, you will be overcome. Overcome with awe and wonder, saturated in mercy and peace that will help you fight through any battle. I long to overwhelm you, so that all you can think of is Me and My love for you. The things of this world will look so small in comparison.

Psalm 27:4   Psalm 118:1, 29

1 Chronicles 16:34

God, Your goodness and kindness is always amazing me. I truly am overwhelmed by who You are. Your great love keeps me in awe of You.

Deep Places

The deep places in Me are always calling to the deep places in you. Anything that seems deep has a feeling of fear and the unknown. But you can rest and know that the deep places in Me have no fear in them. You can jump into the deep things I am calling you to, and with great confidence, know you will land so safely in My arms. Don't stand on the side lines and be a spectator. Don't just watch others experience all that I am. Jump in. my arms are open for you. Faith in Me will allow you to take the steps you need to move toward the edge, and when you get to the edge, lock your eyes on Me and jump!

Psalm 42:7   Hebrews 12:2

Father, I want to always be in the place you call me to. I choose to jump into the deep. I know I will always find You there.

Embrace Each One

Each day is a gift. Within it there are moments that will never come again. What remains with you from each day are the memories you take with you. When each moment, whether good or bad, is spent with Me in mind, then what you take with you from each moment will be in My shadow. Dwell in the secret places with Me in every moment of your life and My shadow will cover your past, present and future. For I hold your days in My hand. Embrace each one. Allow that deep intimate place with Me to breathe life into your every moment. Live out every day knowing My shadow is where you abide. I am always so close to you.

Psalm 91

Thank You that I am tucked tightly under Your shadow. I want everything about my life to be shadowed by Your great love.

Live By Every Word

Trusting in yourself can be a trap. Be careful how wise you think you are. Even your well thought out plans can be deceiving. Spend your time with Me and allow Me to show you things to come. Trust in Me with all your heart. When it is time to make plans, ask Me and acknowledge Me and My wisdom. Seek My word and ways. Search for peace in every event and issue. Take time to listen. Do not move in haste without Me. Your ways simply are not Mine. But I can conform your mind to My word, and My Holy Spirit will teach you all things concerning Me. You can live by every word that comes from Me. Learn of Me.

Proverbs 3:7   Isaiah 55:8   John 14:26

Lord, I know Your ways are so much better than my own. I want so much to follow You so that my every choice is made with Your wisdom.

Waterfall Of My Grace

As you walk through your days in this world and the things of this world would attach themselves to you, know that I provide what you need to wash that away. I have given My sons blood to wash away sins. I have given you My word to wash your mind and soul. Wash daily. Let the water of My Spirit rinse away the anxiety of any moments. You will be refreshed and renewed and white as snow as you stand under the waterfall of My grace and truth. Let truth be the antiseptic that causes any infectious lie not to take root in your heart. Apply the bandage of grace and mercy; be cleansed every day for a new start.

1 John 1:7   Ephesians 5:26

Wash me. Wash me clean. Wash away my anxious ways. Wrap me in truth and mercy. Lord I want to start each day new with You.

My Nearness

Draw very near to me. You need My Presence with you. When your heart is troubled or seems totally overwhelmed, you need My nearness. Even though I am always near you, you fail to recognize how close My closeness is. No matter where you are, I am with you. You may feel unstable or shaken by your circumstances, but if you will stay close to Me, you will not be overcome. No one is capable of being as close to you as I can. No one can provide the security and satisfaction that I can. What your soul longs for, it will truly find when you draw close to Me and let Me draw close to you. For you see, My nearness is your good.

Psalm 73:28   Deuteronomy 31:8

Lord, keep me mindful of Your nearness. I will never be alone. You are always near me. You are so good to me.

Promises In Action

You can trust Me. As sure as the sun rises and sets, you can trust Me. The promises I have made to you are forever settled. I will not go back on My word. I will not allow My word to go unfulfilled. I will watch and stand guard over My words to you to make sure they perform what I send them to do. I have sent My words and promises to sustain and heal you. I have given you My words to strengthen and revive you. So allow My promises to perform for you. Watch and see if they will not obey and accomplish what I have sent them to do. You can watch My promises in action and enjoy the benefits of a life spent trusting Me and My words.

Psalm 119:89 Jeremiah1:12

Psalm 119:50

God, Your word never ceases to amaze me. Knowing you watch over Your word, and that it is active, makes me want to know it more and love You more! Revive me with Your Word.

Only One Wonderful You

I don't ask you imitate anyone but Me. When you long to be like anyone else it will only bring unnecessary strain on your life. And as hard as you try to accomplish what I have given to another, just to be like them, you will never be satisfied. Know in your heart that you have been fashioned and uniquely designed. If you strive to be another then this world will miss having the you that I created. The you I created has a purpose to fulfill. You will find this true and pure self when your soul says "yes" to Me and stops comparing. When delighting yourself in Me becomes more than a song, and when you accept that you are wonderfully made, then you will be free to be the only one wonderful you.

Psalm 139:14 Jeremiah 29:11

Father, I choose to accept that You designed and made me in Your plan. I yield to delighting myself in You. I truly want what You want for me.

Release My Joy

Enter My courts with your praise. Come before Me with singing. I delight in hearing you coming in. I long to dwell in your praises; fill the atmosphere around you with joyful singing. Allow gladness to push out sorrow. You have the ability in Me to cause the very air around you to be permeated with My Presence. I not only am in you, I am all around you. Release My joy and allow it to attract others. Allow your heart to sing even when no sound comes out. I can still hear it. Breathe in My presence and breathe out My praise. It is a good thing to give thanks to Me and to sing praise to Me. You set Me in motion.

Psalm 100:4   Psalm 96:1

Father, I want to be a sound of praise to You. I want my life to be a love song for You. Help me release joy and set You into motion.

An Everlasting Covenant

My love cannot be removed from you. It is not something you can walk away from. You cannot set it aside and pretend it does not exist. You can't sin it away or push it away. You see, My love was given as an everlasting covenant to you. Once you receive and accept that My love is yours, you will discover that it is truly what brings you life; a life that desires to please the One who loves you most. All of the characteristics of My love, I will develop in you, if you will allow it. In love, I will bear all things with you as you grow. When My love begins to grow in you and show through you, My heart is glad because I know your faith in Me will work by this love.

1 Corinthians 13   Galatians 5:6

Develop your love in me, Jesus. Grow in me who You are. I want my faith to work and I know faith works by Your love. Thank You for loving me.

The Melodies of Heaven

You are My instrument of peace. Just as a musical instrument is played by a musician and the sound is heard by all, you are My instrument of peace. I will tune you so that kindness flows from your sound. There will be joy that will permeate each word from you. I will begin to play upon your heart and allow you to hear the melodies of heaven. When chaos and confusion break out around you, I will cause peace to flow from you. When fear rushes in on you, I will assure you that My peace and love in you will cast it far away from you. Allow Me to tune you and train you as My instrument of peace that I can use to play My songs of deliverance through.

2 Timothy 2:21   John 14:27

I surrender myself to be used as Your instrument of peace to all those around me. Tune me and train me to sound out deliverance and joy.

My Plan Still Remains

Even in difficult places where dreams seem gone and goals seem lost, My plan still remains. When it strains you to make sense of anything around you, and hopes seem shattered like broken glass, My plan still remains. When it tempts you to blame Me and ask Me "why", My plan still remains. Surrender to the giving in and fall into Me. Like clay, surrender to the potter's hands; I want to mold you. All of the processes are not pleasant and comfortable; the twisting and turning, pressing and forming all work together for your good. If you will love Me and trust Me, I know who I am making in you. The mold is very secure and sure. Allow Me to press you into the image of My son.

Jeremiah 29:11   Isaiah 64:8

Lord, help me remain yielded to Your gentle hands. I know Your plan is what I really want for my life. Mold me, Great Potter, into Your image.

Stay Open

A willingness to listen to Me must be a steady stream in your life. There is a fine line between making your own plans and listening to Mine. Even though the plans you make for this day may be good in every way, do not allow that to close your ears to Me. Even in those days, I may change and shift things around. Stay open for My voice to lead you differently. If I do, you can rest assured it will be for your good and also for the good of others. I do all things good, so that means that if you allow Me to work and speak through you then all you do and say will be good. Your expectation may be good and Godward but even still be sensitive to My leading.

Isaiah 30:21   John 10:27   Isaiah 26:9

Father, today I choose to lean into listening carefully for You. I don't ever want the business of my life to cause me not to hear Your voice. I want to listen for Your voice first, before all others.

Remain Flexible

Stay flexible My child. Be at peace and rest. Nothing catches Me off guard. Keep your feet firmly planted so your spirit can be flexible and move with My Spirit. I desire for you to be able to run with Me and shift and change with Me, but yet all the while, be firmly planted in My word. The security of your foundation is vital to what you do with Me. The bedrock of who I am must be what holds you steady. The assurance of My love is your security. When you feel shaken or unsteady, I will be your high tower. Let Me whisper in your ear My desires for you. Remain flexible for Me to My Spirit can move you.

Ephesians 3:17 Psalm 16:8

Psalm 18:2

Father I choose to keep my feet firmly planted in You. I want to be free to move with Your Spirit. I don't want to miss anything you have for me.

Weariness Into Rest

Don't grow weary while carrying out My will for you. Your heart and your flesh will fail you so many times. They will talk you into believing things that are not truth. Your flesh will have you hope for a life that I never planned for you. False expectations can be planted in your heart by trying to figure everything out yourself. I never meant that for you. I long for you to have a life with fullness of joy while I carry your cares and burdens. The season for reaping what you have sown will surely come. Wait on Me. Worship Me. Renew your strength. Run toward the rewards for your labor. Turn weariness into rest in Me.

Galatians 6:9,1 Peter 5:7, Psalm 73:26

Lord, when I get tired and weary I want to quit. But You are always there calling me to come to You. Thank You for always, always, always being here for me.

Walk It Out

Oh what great joy you give Me, child. My eyes are on you and My ears are open to your voice. Come before Me and live. I know your coming in and your going out. My ear bends your way when you call My name. My arms are not short that they cannot reach you. Live out this day before Me. I will not take My eyes off of you. Like rain falls down, and flows down the mountain streams, so My love will saturate your entire being. This is how I enable you to walk in My love. First, you let Me pour My love on you, and then when you are totally full and drenched in My love, then and only then, can you walk it out before this world.

Psalm 32:8   Psalm121:8

Isaiah 59:1

Thank You for the security of Your great love for me. I love being Your child. Thank You for watching over me and never leaving me.

Trusted Friend

Always know you can share your deepest feelings with Me. I am your trusted friend. My ears are open to you. I didn't come to condemn you. I don't desire that you think of Me as a critical judge. My desire is for your friendship and love; I am a helper. Ask Me to help and then allow Me to do what only I can do. There isn't anything too hard for Me. Even when you cannot see and your faith feels very weak, you can rest your heart in knowing that I change not. Weariness is never in Me, so I never get tired of being here for you. There is no other friend like Me for you. I cherish our every moment together and I choose to help you fulfill what I created you to do and who I created you to be.

John 3:17   Jeremiah32:2

Philippians 1:6   John 15:15

You are the perfect example of a true friend. You are so good and kind to me, I love my relationship with You! Teach me how to be a good friend.

Warrior Of Peace

When the war between your flesh and your spirit seems to turn into an intense battle, you will find My peace standing at the door of your mind like a warrior in full armor. If you will allow this warrior of peace to have its perfect fight against fears and doubts, it will wield the sword of My perfect love that will destroy what is not of Me. I desire your mind to rest in perfect peace so that all your thoughts can be on Me and of Me. The enemy will fight for rights that only you can give to him. If he wins the territory of your mind, your struggle will increase. Trust peace to stand guard at the entrance of your thoughts, for I am the Prince of Peace, and My kingdom is one of perfect peace and rest.

Philippians 4:7   Isaiah 26:3

Father, today I choose to allow peace to guard my mind. Thank You for Your gift of Jesus, who is my peace. He is my Prince of Peace. I can rest in His kingdom of peace.

Be All Here

The unknown of tomorrow is in My hands. Cast aside the worry of the things and times you cannot see yet and be all here today. This day was made to rejoice in, not fret in. This day was made like no other and will never come again. Your negative words and thoughts waste precious moments that can be spent in encouragement and praise. You add nothing to your life by surrendering to anxiety and harsh words to self and others. But, oh the joy you can add to your own life and to others if your lips speak kindness and praise. Spend this day giving kindness away. It is the sweet fruit of My Spirit that always leaves you wanting more! My lovingkindness is better than life!

Psalm 118:24 Matthew6:27
Galatians 5:22-23

Lord, I want to be all here today. I choose to be full of kindness and encouragement to others. Thank You for the gift of this day!

Great Worth and Value

You are My treasured one, My child. When I formed you, I was not confused. When I placed in you all the things that make you unique, I had a reason. You are perfect for Me to live through. My light can shine perfectly through you. Every ability that you possess is one I can use. Every person you do life with needs Me. If you will yield to My biddings, and the voice of My Spirit, you will be totally amazed at what I can and will do though you. Keep your ears tuned to My voice and your eyes open to My promptings. Move with Me. You have great worth and value to Me and to others. I know; I made you a wonderful treasure.

Ephesians 2:10   _Isaiah 30:21_

Father, it is so humbling to know You made me so unique; That I am Your treasure, full of all that You are. My significance is in You. Your opinion is all that matters.

Ever Mindful

Don't forget all I have done for you. Never stop replaying over and over again the many times you have seen Me answer your prayers. Remind yourself again and again of the cross and the price paid there for you. Be in constant awareness that you have been bought with the price of blood. Be ever mindful of the many times My deliverance has snatched you from the plan of the enemy. Muse on the grace that I have freely offered when you turned away from My ways. Meditate on My goodness and let thanksgiving always be on your lips. Do these things and you will stay in perfect peace because your mind will be on Me.

Isaiah 26:3   Exodus 20:2

1 Corinthians 11:24

Lord, never let me forget all You have done. I choose to think on Your goodness and remember that there is no one like You in all the earth.

Come... Stay

Come sit with Me a while. I have a shelter you can rest in, that will cover you. I will be your hiding place. You are free to come in silence and simply rest. You don't have to speak for Me to know your heart. I will always be a safe place for you to find refuge. Just be still and know that I am your God, and I am here. My nearness is always good for your soul. I will always be close enough to lean on. Rest; I will keep My eyes on you. As you abide in My shelter, I will protect and defend you from the enemy. I will even send angels to watch over you. As you rest, I will revive your spirit and renew your strength. Come... stay.

Psalm 61:4   Psalm 27:5

Psalm 91:11

God, I love that you are always so near to me. Thank You for angels, hiding places, and shelter. I love my moments with You!

The Well Within

Keep your gaze on Me when you are feeling weak and weary. I am your strength. When your eyes fall to the ground and look at your circumstances, you can lose your footing. I didn't say that I would only be your strength when you are weak I will also be your strength when you feel strong. It is then that you need the strength to keep your eyes and heart toward Me most and not on yourself. My strength is a supernatural part of Me that walks hand in hand with My grace. It is always available for you. Draw it up from the well within you. There is always more than enough and it will never run out.

2 Corinthians 12:9   Psalm 31:4

Psalm 18:1

Lord, You truly are my strength. Your grace is always more than enough. I choose to receive the strength You are providing and walk in Your fullness.

Loneliness, The Enemy's Playground

Loneliness is not a part of My plan for your life. Being alone is something that should only be by your choice. I have set the lonely in family. My family. So, as true brothers and sisters in Me, see to it that no one is lonely. Don't think so highly of yourself that you are not willing to reach out and provide family for others. Love one another as I have loved you. I promised to never leave you and to walk with you. Walk with each other, arm in arm. Be a representation of Me and My character. Many reach out for love and acceptance. I will fulfill their longings through you. Loneliness is the enemy's playground. Help Me rescue the lonely ones from his plan.

Psalm 68:6   Matthew 7:12

Father, help me notice the lonely. Give me Your eyes and Your heart to see what You see and what You feel. I need to be more like You.

Embrace The New

Do not get stuck in a rut, child. The only thing that remains the same and will never change is Me and My word. So that leaves you free to change. My word and My Spirit are in constant communion to shift you toward My ways. There are a lot of the ways of men in the past generations that are good. The traditions of men can be good if they are of Me. But I do not desire you cling so tightly to the past that you cannot see Me today. Open your eyes and I will show you wonderful things you know not of. And if you know not of them now then that means they will be new. Embrace the now I bring. Behold old things are passed away and all things are new. Hold tight to the unchanging word of God and embrace the new He brings to you.

Isaiah 43:19   Jeremiah 33:3
1Peter 1:23

Thank You that Your word never changes. I desire you to shift me and guide into new life with You. I want to always press forward into Your plans for me.

I Sit On The Praises

Sing to Me the song in your heart. All of creation sings their songs to Me. Join in, allow the depths of your heart to be released in melody. All sound from you, in praise to Me, is precious and lovely. No one's ears matter but Mine. Let the words from your mouth and the meditation of your heart be pleasing to me. Come before Me with joyful songs. A joyful heart is attractive and will draw others to you. Likewise, you can repel others by the sounds and words from your mouth. Allow My Spirit to use you to 'woo' and draw others with the songs that come from you. Encourage one another; build one another up with songs of praise to Me. Make My glory known. I sit on the throne of the praises of My people.

Psalm 96:1   Psalm 19:14

Colossians 3:16

God, I want whatever comes from my mouth to be pleasing to You and edifying to others. I choose to praise You and give all the glory to You.

I Chose You

There are no buildings that house Me anymore. I used to abide in a tent or a temple for men to come to, but not any longer. I have chosen you to be My dwelling place. I have chosen you to be My Holy of Holies. You see, if I dwell in a tent or building, men must come to Me, but by dwelling in you, you carry Me to men. You present Me to the world. They get to see who I am by knowing you. They are able to see My compassion for them by seeing yours. No building can show My love and forgiveness. My kindness and grace is not in a window or a door. I chose you with hands and feet, arms and eyes, heart and spirit to express who I am to this world. Come and learn of Me so you can present Me for who I really am.

1 Corinthians 6:19   2 Corinthians 3:2-3

Father, it humbles me to know You live in me so those around me can know You. I so long to represent you well. Live through me, Lord.

Plant Your Feet Firm

When My winds of change blow around you, and you feel shifts and movements all around, plant your feet firm. For when seasons of change come, they are always for your good. A season of planting and growing means plowing and hard labor; pulling up weeds and watering. The harvest is so joyful with full enjoyment of tasting what you have worked for. Then the time of pruning is to assure that you will be strong for an even greater harvest to come. I am the vinedresser, you are the vine. Trust Me in the seasons of your life. I know what will help you to be strong and fruitful. I will care for you with a watchful eye. I can help you become like a tree planted by the water whose leaves never wither.

Luke 6:48   John 15:1   Psalm 1:3

Father, help me stand firm and yield to You ways in my life. I trust Your unfailing love to strengthen me as I grow up in You.

Guard Against Pride

Search your soul for the places that pride has crept in. I do not want to have to resist you in any way. This attitude of pride has caused so many of My children to stumble and fall. Pride will cause you to think higher of yourself than you should. It will cause you to think you can live without Me. The enemy just waits for a foothold to grab you in this area of pride. He knows I resist the proud. If you become puffed up with pride then he knows you will have a hard time engaging Me. I love you enough to let you make the choice. But oh, child, guard against pride with all your heart, soul, and spirit. Pride goes before a fall. I can keep your feet from ever stumbling.

1 Peter 5:5   Romans 12:3

Proverbs 16:18   Psalm 56:13

Lord, keep me from pride. Help me recognize it quickly in myself. I never want you to resist me. Keep my feet from stumbling as I humbly walk before You.

Pot Holes

On the road before you there are places that appear to be pot holes, a mere bump in the road. Do not be deceived. These pot holes can be deep pits that have no end, falling into a darkness that will try to take My life from you. Do not trust your eyes of the flesh to discern what you see. Seek Me first. Allow the light of My Word to guide your steps. The enemy is deceiving and will twist the truth that you know. Take heed, lest you fall. Walking with Me I will not allow your foot to stumble. Do not turn your eyes to another. Be sure footed and mature in your walk with Me, so that others can walk after you and not stumble.

1 Peter 5:8   Psalm 119:105

Hebrews 12:2

Father, help me keep my eyes on You. Shine Your light so bright that I can plainly see any trap of the enemy. Thank You for Your love.

Shine

Your life is seen and read by all who know you. Your actions will always speak louder than your words. Hide My words in your heart. Learn of Me, and allow Me to live in you and through you, so that others can know Me. Let your words be My words. Love when love is not expected. Give grace when grace is undeserved. Offer forgiveness to all who have wronged you. How will they know Me? I've made you a light; A city on a hill. As a lighthouse shines the way to safety, so you should shine. Shine through the fog and the storms that darkens the way. Never let My light go out in you for there is always someone in stormy waters trying to see the way home.

2 Corinthians 3:2-3   Psalm 86:11

Isaiah 60:1

Lord, I want to always be the one that points people toward You. I want to represent Your character and Your nature. Shine through me so others can find You.

My Joy

I have set a joy before you just as I did for My son. A hope of an eternal life spent with Me. I desire you to embrace this joy and allow it to strengthen your inner man. When My joy is ever before you, it will produce a supernatural endurance that will enable you to be strong. This joy is the power of My might. It is not anything you can find in this world. Nothing has the power to strengthen you like My joy. The fullness of My joy that I long to fill you with is found only in My presence. The joy that will cause you to endure hardships and trials, heartbreak and pain, is only found in My presence. In My presence is where you belong. Be strong in the Lord.

Ephesians 6:10   Psalm 16:11

Thank You for the joy I find in Your presence. I love being with You. Infuse me with your strength and make me more like You.

Live In My Embrace

My arms are always wide open for you to run into. My embrace is not only here for you when you are down, but I love to embrace you in your happiest of moments. An embrace is given in celebrations, as well as, in sorrow; in greetings, as well as, goodbyes. But My embrace around you is constant. All you have to do is receive My touch. The love I have for you is so strong that I want you to live in My embrace. Live from me holding you close to Me. You will be so sheltered in My love and you will see life from My presence. I will not allow you to be shaken or insecure. Rest in My embrace, I am your Lord.

Luke 15:20   *Jeremiah 31:3*

Father, teach me and show me what it means to live Your constant embrace.

Be Refreshed

I am bringing times of refreshing. Time to wash off the grime of the battle and dip yourself into the refreshing waters of My word. A time where your battle cries can turn into songs of worship and praise. I will lead you beside still, refreshing waters. I will cause you to lie down in green pastures. I have promised to supply your every need even before you can ask. So, be refreshed in the stillness and the quiet. Do not strive, but receive. You will gain a knowing that I am God. I will refresh your mind and renew your spirit. You will be clean and ready for all your days ahead.

Psalm 23: 1-4   Acts 3:20

Father, I receive refreshing from You. Revive my spirit and my soul today.

I Go Before You

For you, today is new. Yet, I have seen this day because I go before you. Because I walk before you, if you keep your eyes on Me, then you will walk in the ways and the path I have made for you. By following Me, I can already push aside anything that would be in your way. With your hand in Mine, I can keep you on course. I won't allow you to stumble when your eyes and focus are on Me. I don't want you to be tossed about by winds that would try to knock you down. So, as I go before you, hold tight to Me and set your affections on Me. With every step we take, we will gain new ground so others can follow.

Hebrews 12:2 Ephesians 4:14

Lord, thank You that I do not ever have to walk alone. I love the constancy of Your presence. I choose today to hold tight to Your unchanging hand.

Chosen You To Be Mine

Never cease to marvel at the greatness of My love. It is unending and unsearchable. I have given you this time on earth to discover and accept all of who I am. I have given you a grace to put your faith in. I long for your choices to be made with Me in mind; For every decision you make, to be carefully made, with the wisdom I provide for you. I have chosen you to be Mine; you are My child, and heir to all I have. Now, My delight is you choosing Me to give your devotion to. I promise never to leave you or forsake our relationship. Promise Me the same. Give yourself to Me as freely as I have given Myself to you.

Galatians 4:7   Song Of Solomon 2:16

God, Your incredible love draws me. Your arms wrap around Me and keep me. I surrender in total devotion to You and You alone.

We Walk Together

Call to Me and I will answer. I am always a present help. I care about what concerns you. I have called you My friend and I care about you like a devoted and true friend. You can share your most intimate thoughts with Me and trust Me with them. I know your heart and I share My heart with you. Just as two friends walk arm in arm, sharing with each other every detail of their lives, so we walk together, you and I. So come walk with Me. Lock your arm into Mine and let's share our lives together. I care about you and all that makes you who you are. I love being with you, I call you friend.

Psalm 34:4   1 Peter 5:7

John 15:15

Lord, thank You for being my best friend!

Harvest Will Surely Come

There are times you will give even if it hurts. There are times you will love even if no love is returned. During these painful moments, trust Me and know that I understand. Sacrificial giving and loving is a supernatural way of living. Nothing births life more than these. No selfishness lives in a true heart that gives and loves. Selfish gain falls away and seeds for harvest are planted. Although you may never get to eat the full fruit of seeds sown, the harvest will surely come to full bloom. So, when you are tempted to withhold love and not give freely, remember that I completely love you and give you My very life.

Luke 6:38   Genesis 8:22

Father, teach me the full meaning of planting seeds of love and the harvest it brings.

Destiny Is In Me

I have set destiny before you. I know the plans I have for you. This plan and destiny will pull you to it like a force of gravity. There is always a bidding and a drawing inside your soul that beckons you onward. Draw near to Me and I will draw near to you. Don't allow the enemy to entice you with the lusts of this world. Fix your eyes on Me. I will never lead you astray. As you walk toward Me you will walk right into your destiny and My plans for you. In this world you will have tribulations. Troubles and trials will try to knock you down, but walk on with great joy knowing I have

Jeremiah 29:11   James 4:8

John 16:33

Today I choose to keep my eyes on You, Lord. I choose to keep walking toward my destiny in You.

Spill Out In Full

When hope seems lost and all of the darkness presses on the light that you have, still your soul and lean. Lean, with full weight of despair onto My grace. Allow the emptiness inside to spill out in full and then trust Me to fill the void with hope. Hope, to see again what was stolen so violently from you. Let me give you eyes that see in faith what you cannot see. Let me bathe you in My love that hopes and bears all things. Know that hope is truly never completely lost, it just gets covered up by the cares of this life. Put your hope in Me. To ever put it in anything or anyone else will only leave you empty. Lift up your head; put your trust in Me.

Psalm 40:10   1Corinthians 13:7

Psalm 42:5

God, I am leaning into You with all I am. I know my hope is found in You. Help me hope again.

You Carry My Name

Stand tall; take courage. Be brave and not afraid, for I am mighty and I am in you. I am greater in you than the one in the world. My name has been given to you and is above every name in heaven and on earth. Let your eyes of faith see your enemy's tactics with their knees bowed to Me. All the spirits of darkness, that do the bidding of the father of lies, will bow to Me. Never bow to them; you are greater. You carry My name. You have keys to My kingdom, and no one can hold you back. You are an heir with the rights to enter boldly into My presence. My name is your key, My blood was the price, and My presence is your home.

1 John 4:4   Philippians 2:9

Hebrews 4:16

Jesus, You make me brave!

Let's Talk

Don't worry about anything, but pray about everything. Worry is when you are talking to yourself; prayer is when you are talking to Me. Worry is when you are busy in your mind trying to figure out the future; prayer is when you can experience peace in your mind knowing and trusting that I hold your every tomorrow. Worry is when you allow small problems to become large unclimbable mountains. Prayer is where the problems stay small in the shadow of the vastness of who I am. Worry will steal away your health, your joy and your life. In prayer, you will be assured that I am here and will bring healing, abundant joy, and everlasting life. Don't worry My child. Let's talk.

Matthew 6:25-34 Philippians 4:6

Father, today I choose to talk to you about everything and not give in to worry! Help me make this my lifestyle.

With All Your Heart

You will find in this life that your heart is not meant to belong to another. This is why I said to love Me with all your heart. Don't freely give portions of your heart away to have it trampled and abused; Only trust Me with it. I have asked you to love your neighbor as yourself, but your heart belongs to Me. I am so jealous of your heart, I long to be the one who satisfies your very soul. I yearn for your thoughts to be on Me. For My love is deep for you and as wide as the heavens. My heart of compassion is yours. All I ask is that you love Me with all your heart, soul, mind and strength. I will withhold no good thing from you.

Deuteronomy 6:5   Matthew 22:37

Psalm 84:11

God, I will only give my heart to You. Fill me with Your love so I can give Your love to others.

I Will Answer

You can know that when your voice cries out to Me, My ears hear you. I will answer you and come to your rescue. When your enemies come against you, I am here with you strengthening you in your inner man. I have given you a shield of salvation that will protect you when you raise it up and know its abilities. I will never leave you helpless or without hope. I can reach down and pull you out of deep waters and rescue your very soul. Walk blameless in Me and I will clothe you with strength. I will widen the place beneath your feet and cause the crooked places to become straight. I would not have you defeated by any enemy that has come against you. I will always fight for you and with you.

Psalm 50:15   Deuteronomy 1:30

2 Samuel 22:36

Lord, thank You for equipping me with the tools I need for any battle. Thank You for always fighting for me and with me.

Washed and Refreshed

Just as rain showers wash over and refresh the land, My word comes to wash and refresh you. When you hear My words as they gently drop like raindrops in your heart, you are watered and renewed. Bathe in the pools of revelation I give you so that your heart will be cleansed and pure. Soak yourself in My presence and let My words penetrate every cell of your body and bring healing. Submerge your mind and allow all your thoughts to be renewed and washed clean. My word provides all your soul is hungry for. Great showers of blessings are waiting for you every time you give yourself to washing and renewing in My words. I am always speaking.

Ephesians 5:26   Psalm 107:20

Romans 12:2

Lord, Your words are light and life to me. I choose to delight myself in Your word. Renew me daily by Your great word. I love Your word, God.

Let Go Of Yesterday

Allow the pain of yesterday's mistakes to be dipped into My steadfast love, mixed with the new mercy of today. So that your eyes can see, and your ears hear, what I have for all your tomorrows. When the disappointment and discouragement cause your heart to give up its hope, realize that the simple turning of your eyes back to me can call hope back in order. Set your affections on Me, and I will help heal past hurts and mistakes, and cause beauty to arise from the ashes. I know My plans for you and there is always a future and a hope. Swim in My mercy stream and let go of yesterday. Today is a new day.

Philippians 3:13   Lamentations 3:23

Isaiah 61:3

Thank You, Lord, that my yesterdays can be immersed in the mercy of today. Thank You, for making all things new. I know You work all things for my good, because, I love You, and You have called me for Your purpose.

Stay Alert

Battles are not for you to fight alone. True battles in your life need a strategic battle plan. When your enemy is already standing with his sword drawn and ready to defeat you, it is too late to go to the drawing table of the spirit and strategize a plan of war. Today, and every day, is the time to listen for the voice of the Captain of the Hosts and clothe yourself with the armor of the Lord. Don't wait until you are being hit with the arrows of the enemy's bow to prepare yourself. Put on your helmet of salvation and hold your shield of faith with a firm grip. Gird yourself with truth and walk in the protection gospel of peace. Stay alert. Be aggressive toward the fight. You be the one with sword in hand, ready for battle, and I will go before you.

Ephesians 6:10-18

Lord, I know there is never a time to take my ease. You provide a way for me to be all ready to battle the enemy. I choose to stay alert and ready.

Prayers Never Die

I am listening. My ears are open to your cries. I am answering your deepest heart groaning. I know what you need even before the request leaves your lips. I assure you, I am well able to do the impossible. As bright light blinded Saul and changed his heart toward Me; likewise, I can swiftly move and change the ones you bring before Me. For I am the one who is ever interceding for You to the Father. Don't grow weary, for even if you never see your request come to past in the natural, your prayers never die. I will answer. Receive My answers by faith and not by sight. Trust Me. Nothing is impossible for Me.

Matthew 6:8   Hebrews 7:25

James 5:16

Father, I understand my ways are not Your ways. Thank You for seeing what I can't and answering in ways that sometimes I don't understand. Nothing is too hard for You.

More Than Enough

I am more than enough. In this life of desires and expectations, there is a constant reaching for more. There is a fast pace of longing, and searching, and grabbing for what might satisfy for a short while. My ways for you is to experience the realness of the promise that I am more than enough. More than enough love for your heart to be secure in. More than enough healing for your body and your mind. More peace than you are capable of walking in. More grace than this life can hold. I give good gifts. I pour out blessings. I open the windows of heaven over you. I am the exceedingly abundant one. I do not withhold when you are walking with Me. There will always be more than enough.

Ephesians 3:20   Psalm 84:11

Oh My Lord, to me, You are more than enough!

I Will Remind You

I am in the little things. As you rush through your day I am with you. Don't miss all the ways I will remind you of My presence and who I am: the song bird in the tree; the light breeze against your face. The vastness of the sky above you and the very dirt you stand on will proclaim the glory of who I am. The very breath of air in your lungs today is a reminder that the purpose I have for you on the earth is not completed. Breathe in this life today and exhale the joy of knowing I am in you and all around you. You can see Me if your eyes are focused on all the ways I say I love you.

Jeremiah 29:13   Luke 11:9

Ephesians 1:23

Lord, You fill all things with Yourself. Open my eyes to see You and Your great love for me.

Time Is My Gift

Time is a gift from Me. You cannot make time. I made time and gave it to you as a gift to be received. You get to choose what you will do with this precious gift. Many gifts I give are wasted and never used for My purposes. Time is the one gift most often abused. There are many thieves and robbers wanting to take this gift from you. The enemy is on a constant mission to steal, kill and destroy. Hold on to this precious gift. Live in thankfulness of every moment given. Learn to recognize the enemy's subtle ways of creeping in and taking your time. Choose wisely who you share your time with. Time is in My hands and is My gift to you. Embrace each moment.

Ephesians 5:16   John 10:10

Psalm 31:15

Father, help me to be aware every moment of every day that each second of time I have is precious and can be spent loving You.

For My Pleasure

I am a jealous God. I am constantly showing you My love. I am always speaking and singing over you the unmeasurable affection I have for you. I created you for My pleasure and for our friendship. Your heart was made to love Me first and to allow love for others to flow from our love. I am jealous when you seek the things of this world because I desire you to seek My kingdom first. You are invited by Me, the King, to seek My entire kingdom. To search out every part of it and all it contains. It's all yours! And in your seeking you will find all you need is added to you. Enjoy the search; seek and find. Seek, and you will find Me.

Jeremiah 29:13   Matthew 6:33

Father, walk me through Your kingdom and show me Your kingdom ways so that I can walk with You.

Run Into Me

Come in from the storm, I am your shelter. When the rumble of thunderous problems sound in the distance, prepare to run to My shelter. When sudden situations strike like an angry lightning bolt that shakes your inner man, already be on your way to Me. Being a shelter for your soul is a promise I have made to you. I will cover you and protect you. But you must come and hide here in Me. I cannot make you come. I don't desire you to be overcome by any storm of this life; I long to be your place of covering and safety. Run into Me and will overshadow you with all that I am.

Psalm 91:1-2   Proverbs 27:5-6

Lord, thank You for being my safe hiding place.

My Kingdom Will Come

When the enemy rushes in on you in subtle or not so subtle ways, I will rise against him. For My name has the power over all. It is the name that is above every name. No terrorist or demon in hell can defeat My chosen. My kingdom will come and My will be done on earth as it is in heaven. Remain humble and steadfast in your days. Hide My words in your heart so that the sin that wants to tangle you into confusion will have no place in you. Fight back with your worship, proclaiming the goodness of who I am. There is no defeat for you as long as you are in Me. Not even death can keep you from life. The battle belongs to Me. I will prevail. I am the first and the last, the only true God.

Philippians 2:9-11 Psalm 119:11 Revelation 22:13

God, You are my God. Your name is great and greatly to be praised! I stand in awe of You.

It's How They Will Know

I never meant for you to walk alone. You are a very unique and valuable part of My body. My blood flows to you so that you can live and move and have your being through Me. You exist so all of the other parts of My body can function well. This is why I continually say to encourage one another and lift one another up. You are here for the strength and support of those around you. You need each other. You are My body on the earth to be seen and read by all. Don't pull away from each other; don't separate yourself, for when you do My body looks deformed and disfigured. But how wonderful and pleasant it is when My body walks in unity. This is how they will know you are Mine if you love one another.

Acts 17:28

1 Corinthians 12:27   Hebrews 10:25

Lord, Thank You for my brothers and sisters in Christ. Help me be the encourager that they need.

I Am Not Napping

I am working in ways you cannot see. I have things in motion that will come together in My timing. Even when your eyes are weary from the waiting on Me, I am still busy working all things together for your good, because I know you love Me and have accepted the call of My name. I will never grow tired or weary. While I watch over you, I am not napping. I am always directing your steps and shining light for your path. I am making sure there is a way of escape should you fall into a trap in those moments when you take your eyes off of Me. My arms are always open wide and My grace is always sufficient for you. So, as you walk through today, know that I am working for your good.

Romans 8:28   Psalm 121:4

2 Corinthians 12:9

Father, thank You that I can have confidence that You are always working things out for my good.

Captured

I have surrounded you on every side. There is no place to run or hide. You have been overthrown; you can no longer be the most powerful and wise in your own eyes. I have set an ambush against your flesh and have declared all-out war. I have sought you by My love that knew you before you were born. I have surrounded you with grace that is jealous for your soul. My mercy that flows from My mercy seat longs to capture your very heart. And as you drop to your knees in total surrender, My lovingkindness will overwhelm your very being. I long to take you captive. Not to make you prisoner, but to set you free. Free to be Mine. Lavished in My goodness and My love for you. Surrender all.

Galatians 5:1   Jeremiah 31:3

Lord, I surrender.

Listen For My Voice

Your faith in Me will grow as you learn to listen. Make your ears attentive to My wisdom and gain the understanding you seek. I am not silent and I do not hide Myself from you. I am in plain view and My voice is clear. Train your ears to be turned to My words. When you listen and you hear, then your faith will grow. I will speak to you treasures of My word that will sustain you. I will unlock mysteries and reveal revelation that your heart will cling to. I will allow you to see and know Me and My ways. So, be alert to My Spirit. Listen for My voice. Incline your ear to My sayings. Hold them close to your heart; they will bring life and health to you.

Proverbs 4:20 Romans 10:17

1 Corinthians 2:10

God, I choose to listen for Your voice today. Your words are my life and my health.

My Disciple

You were born for such a time as this. I have placed within you greatness and favor. I have chosen you to live in Me and for Me. All around you people are searching for Me, people that don't even believe I am real. But I have set you in their midst, and placed My Spirit on you, that you will show forth My goodness. It matters how you live, for your life is being read like a book. All who see you and know you will learn of Me and My ways. As you walk blameless before Me you will attract the brokenhearted. As My love flows from you, the hurting will make their way to you. It is Me that makes you attractive to this world. It is My favor that draws your destiny to come. Choose to be My disciple, My representative and follow Me.

Esther 4:14   Isaiah 60:1-2

Psalm 1

Lord, live in me and through me. I want to be a true disciple of you.

Drink Until You Are Full

When your heart becomes weary in the battle and the weight gets too heavy to carry, remember that I am with you. When sadness shapes your days and tears flow freely, I am here. This world has its troubles and trials. It can cause hearts to break and pressure that can feel crushing. But in every moment of weakness I am near. In every thought that questions "why?" I am speaking peace. Don't let your heart be troubled. Trust in Me who promised to never leave you abandoned. Weeping may last for a night but My joy will come. Because I am with you always, My joy is always present. Draw from the well of joy and gladness and drink until you are full; My joy will chase sorrow and mourning away.

John 14:27   Psalm 30:5   John 4:13-14

Lord, I will always draw my strength from knowing You are with me. You are my joy and gladness.

Keep Moving Forward

Go throughout this day knowing fully that nothing is impossible for Me. Stretch your faith a little farther and reach a little deeper into the well of believing. Against hope, believe in hope. When all seems lost, look once again. When the darkness closes in, push back with the light you have. Don't give in or give up, keep moving forward and step beyond the situation. When you have given in to weariness, lift your head and search for My peace. Grab your unbelief and choke the life out of it; remind yourself Whose you are. Pick up your bow of belief and aim for your destiny. Follow the arrow of possibility for nothing is too hard for Me.

Jeremiah 32:17   Romans 4:18

Hebrews 10:23

Father, today in Jesus' name, I choose to keep believing and press forward because nothing is too hard for You.

A Soldier

I am preparing you for the days ahead of you. I have you in training just like a soldier preparing for battle. You must train to tune your ears to My commands and not the thoughts of your own reasoning. Build yourself up in the spirit so that you are strong and courageous. Learn to use the weapons I give you. Become familiar with them so they are ready at any moment needed. Know your rank and calling, being ready to give account for every move. Defend and encourage your fellow warriors so that together you trust one another as you follow Me. You will never be alone in battle. If you will allow Me to prepare you and train you, then when it is time to fight your eyes will open to see that you are a vital part of the vast army of the Most High.

2 Corinthians 10:4   Ephesians 6:11

Hebrews 12:1

Father, I want to be a soldier for You. Equip me and help me to ready myself for what's ahead.

Slow The Pace Down

Be patient, child. Don't get in a hurry. Be willing to slow the pace down to a steady rest of movement. In your desire to rush, you run past so much. So many opportunities watch you rush right by without as much as a glance. Acknowledge Me in all your ways. Come back to listening. Take the time to listen and I will point out to you what matters for eternity. Your selfish striving and spending will leave you empty and tired. Your worldly desire for more success will cause your heart to wander from Me. So, acknowledge Me and seek Me first. I will add all these other things to you. I will be the One who can make your way prosperous and cause you to have success. So slow the pace down and come to Me and I will give you rest in your doing.

Proverbs 3:5-7   Matthew 6:33 Joshua 1:8

Lord, keep me steady. I long to stay in rest as I do what You have called me to do.

Greater Things

I am able. And through Me, you are able. Your ability in Me and what I can do in you and through you is the way of the supernatural. Your natural mind will not only limit you, it will limit Me. Your mind will reduce Me to the natural. I am not limited to that realm. The very vastness of this universe is Mine. I call the stars by name and yet know the very hairs on your head. That much alone will tell you that you are in the supernatural with Me. My kingdom in you is far greater than your two eyes can see. Yet I call you to a place where your eyes can open to see all the wonders of who I am. I am able, and in Me you are able. Greater things will you do, and greater things yet will you see. For greater am I in you!

Philippians 4:13   1 John 4:4

Jesus, never let me forget that You are able and You are in me!

I Understand

Press into Me. I know you feel like I am not around sometimes. I understand when the weight gets so heavy that you want to say "please, let this cup pass from me". I do understand what it's like to be rejected and hated. I understand what it's like to have your closest friends turn their backs on you. I am a God who truly understands your pain. Learn from Me and in your hard moments, find a place alone with Father. Allow the strength I can give you to refresh your spirit and renew your mind. Let me renew your strength and cause you to soar like eagles! Your pain in My hand will be healed. I will never allow more than you can bear. Press into Me and melt into all I am and be baptized in My goodness.

Hebrews 4:15

1 Corinthians 10:13   1 Peter 5:7

Lord, thank You for caring and for understanding all I go through. I choose to turn to You.

<u>Your Heart Is My Garden</u>

As a gardener watches over his fields, watch over your heart. Break up the hard places that will resist the seed of My word. Pull up the weeds of confusion and ungodly beliefs that choke out the truth. Water the dry places with My love and grace and watch Me cause a soft, workable, pliable place for My seeds to be planted. Guard the tender shoots of My wisdom as they grow into deep rooted revelation that is unshakable. Allow My light to shine and bring strength to every truth planted. Chase away the things that long to steal the seeds and eat the fruit. Your heart is My garden where I plant My word in you. Guard it. Tend to it. Watch over it, and many will eat and be nourished.

Proverbs 4:23 Mark 4:20

heart. I desire to have a heart that is a fruitful garden for You.

Lessons To Be Learned

Tangled up in every messy situation is My grace. It is the gift that helps you comb through every knotted up area that seems impossible. When your mind and will try to figure out and fix the confusion even you yourself get caught in the web. Learn to back away and look through My eyes. Make sure that you are seeking Me first before you jump into tangled webs. Be still. The more you fight and pull the more wrapped up in the problems you get. Step back and ask for wisdom. I will give you all you need. I am generous to show you every step, and patient to lead the way out. You can know there is a way of escape. I always provide one. But the journey to freedom has great lessons to be learned along the way. And I will carry you if necessary.

Hebrews 12:1 James 1:5

1 Corinthians 10:13

Lord, I ask you for Your wisdom. Keep me away from the traps of the enemy. I desire to learn from You!

Seeds

I don't teach you and show you the things I do so that you can keep them to yourself. When you spend time with Me, and I reveal Myself to you, it's like being handed a bag of seeds. You can take these seeds of My character and My revelations and plant them into others. I watch over these precious seeds. Every one of them has life giving power! When you choose to receive these seeds from Me it makes you a witness for Me. You can scatter the seeds of My words to everyone you meet. It is their responsibility to decide whether they receive it or not, not yours. Your faithfulness is all I require of you. Spend this life gathering seeds and sowing them everywhere. I can take it from there. And always know that what you sow, you reap. Sow continually so that the harvest never stops coming in.

John 6:63   Galatians 6:9

Lord, I long to be one who scatters Your seeds into everyone I meet. Cause harvest of who You are to grow.

Eyes On The Road

Be persistent in your pursuit of Me. I am not hard to find. When your feet leave the smooth path and insist on climbing rocky cliffs and tripping into valleys causing you to tumble and fall, it makes you feel that I am hard to seek out. And even though I will be with you as you struggle trying to find your own way, I really do have a smoother path for you to travel. I have roads paved with peace, complete with guard rails and warning signs. But you must keep your eyes on the road. The enemy will cause your eyes to wander and drift into places that are not of Me. Develop a constant awareness of your surroundings. Let no one cause you to stumble. This persistent walk with Me may seem difficult at times, but the abundant life it will give you is My gift with every step you make.

Isaiah 26:3   Psalm 119:15
Psalm 32:8

Lord, I choose to fix my eyes on You. I trust You to lead me and guide me in all I do.

Even Though I Cannot See

Even when you can't see Me, I am moving all around you. There are answers to the prayers you have prayed making their way to you and to the situations that concern you. Don't give up because nothing seems to be changing. Don't allow discouragement to swallow you into a dark hold of depression. Have faith and patience in Me so that My promises can come to you. Allow endurance to have its perfect work in you. You are not forgotten or alone. I have placed ministering angels all around you. The spirit world around you is busy and though your natural eyes may not see this activity, it is still there. Even when unbelief knocks at your mind's door, answer with this: "I am blessed because I believe even though I cannot see"!

James 1:4   John 20:29

Lord, I know that You are always working on my behalf. Help me believe even though I don't see… yet.

Open Your Heart

There is much yet for you to know. As your heart cries out for wisdom and knowledge of me, I will teach you. Open your heart to My word. The depths of the riches you will discover are far greater than the wealth of this world. There is treasure that surpasses that of fine gold and precious stones. Open your heart to know the wisdom that comes from Me is the direct guidance you need for this life. The purpose of this life is not to gain the wealth of this world, but to discover who I am and lay up that treasure in heaven. Life on earth is a short passageway to eternity with Me. Don't be deceived by the temporary wealth of this world that will draw your heart from Me. I will teach you and give you all things pertaining to life and godliness. Enjoy learning of Me; it's eternal.

Psalm 16:16   Matthew 6:20-21
              2 Peter 1:3

Lord, nothing on this earth can satisfy my soul like You.

Fullness Of Joy

I have set before you fullness of joy. This total fullness of everlasting joy is stationed in My presence. I do not ask you to seek Me so that you will struggle and strain to find Me. I invite you to seek Me so that your joy may be full. When you yield yourself into My presence, My joy gives you strength. I don't ask you to be strong and of good courage just so you can fight your battles. I ask you to be strong so you will come into My presence and drink of My joy so then your strength will be made complete. I have set joy before you so you can endure. Endurance is accomplished if your eyes are on the joy in My presence. The road through any hardship is paved with strength and joy if you will let Me walk with you.

John 15:11   Psalm 16:11   Psalm 28:7

God, today I choose to walk with You in Your strength and joy.

Turn Loose

Have you picked up those cares again that you already laid down? Did you cast them on Me and then reel them back again? Turn loose and trust Me. I have heard the deep cries of your heart. I know that when you can't see, you doubt. Believe that I am making a way, even if it doesn't look like there is one. Hold onto My words I have given you, and rest in knowing I am able. So let's try this again... cast your cares on Me and state your thanksgiving to me. When you thank Me for taking the situation you won't try to take it away from Me. Acknowledge with gratitude that you know I care for the things that concern you. They are too heavy for you, so let My strength work all things together for good. Just continue to love Me and trust Me. I am good. Leave it in My very capable hands.

1 Peter 5:7   Philippians 4:6
Psalm 118:1

Lord, forgive me for continually taking back the things I give to You. I know You are good and You deeply care for me.

The Hours Of The Ordinary

Receive My blessing and favor this day. Allow Me to pour out My love to you as you walk through the hours of the ordinary. Swim in My peace that I give to calm your mind. Enjoy My grace that has an endless supply. Be overwhelmed in My goodness that I delight to show you. Let My kindness overshadow any doubts or fears attempting to cripple you. Bathe in the forgiveness of sins so that you are clean and white as snow. So, as you walk out this ordinary day with its ordinary ways, be reminded that I daily desire to load you down with blessing and favor. I desire each day for you to rejoice in yet another day that I have made and fashioned for you. Walk in the joy of My presence and remember Me.

Psalm 68:19

God, thank You for each new day that comes already loaded with blessing to be poured out and received. Thank You!

Be Alert

Be alert and attentive. There are those who are trying to distract your focus. The amount of attention you give them will determine the amount of distraction. When you make a decision to pray and fast, or to set your mind on the ways of My spirit, the enemy will set an ambush. Sometimes He dresses them up in the things our flesh desires most. Underneath the outer beauty can lie a trap that may entangle you and cause you to fall into a deep dark hold. So be alert. Be aware and awake. Be watchful so you will not be ignorant of the enemy's plans. Listen carefully for My voice saying "this is the way, walk in it". I am constant and sure. I set no traps for you. I will only lead you and guide you into all truth. Be wise in the knowledge of My will and your foot will not slip.

1 Peter 5:8   Isaiah 30:21   John 16:13

Father, I choose to stay alert and aware. I will listen and watch for You. You won't let me slip.

<u>Names</u>

I have called you. I have named you. But this world has also named and called you. It puts labels on you that cause you to live under a pressure that I have never intended for you. You also call yourself names that tear down what I am trying to build and establish in you. Tune your ears to Me. I call you lovely. I call you Mine. I call you My friend. I call you altogether beautiful. I call you an overcomer and a great warrior. I call you My favored one. I say you are blessed and you are a blessing. Allow Me to be the one that places labels on you. Agree with me and call yourself by My names for you. My banner over you is love. I call you My beloved, I am yours and you are Mine.

Isaiah 43:1   John 15:15
Song of Solomon 2:4

God, thank You that who I really am is who You say I am. Thank You for affirming me.

My Shadow

I am drawing you into My secret place. This part of Me is open to you as My friend. Our times together here are intimate and transparent. I long to share My heart with you and show you My ways. I will conform you to be like Me when we share together. I long for you to dwell here with Me. Abide here in My shadow. Live in My shadow. This world will make you live in the shadows of false expectations and other people. These shadows cast doubt and unbelief in yourself that you cannot reach beyond. But My shadow assures you that I am near. And when you dwell in My shadow, no other shadow is over you and even the very shadow that comes from you is Me. My shadow becomes your shadow. Abide in Me and cast My shadow on your world.

Psalm 91:1   John 15:7   Psalm 63:7

Father, tuck me in tight under Your shadow and never let me drift from this safe place.

When Light Breaks In

It is My joy to watch you grow in My graces; to see you embrace My words and allow them to mold you and change you, to watch you choose to shift from darkness into My marvelous light. When that light breaks in and your mind becomes renewed, My life begins to take root down deep in your soul. My spirit and your spirit unite in the union of My word and cause My power to shift the atmosphere around you. This is what it means to walk in newness of life. It's in Me that you live and move and have your very life. When this explosion of unity happens, life is birthed again and again. Walk with Me in this life as you choose to let My words grow deep and break up all that is not of Me. My life and light will continually break forth.

3 John 1:4   1 Peter 2:9   Acts 17:28

God, keep changing me. Keep shifting me from darkness to light. I want newness of life to continue to grow in me.

Me Through You

A day of refreshing and renewal is here for you today if you choose to see it and embrace it. I have laid out a path that will show you My never-ending love and faithfulness. I have called you and equipped you specifically for My purposes and My plan. Walk from a rested, refreshed place in Me. Allow My peace to guide you. As others search for Me they are looking for this refreshing peace and unconditional love that I can cause to shine from your life. But if you are worried and confused, and My peace has no place in you, then they will not see Me. So come and let Me refresh you. Let Me tell you of My love and assure you of who I am. Not only will you be renewed, but others will come to be restored by Me through you.

Acts 3:20   Matthew 11:28   Ephesians 4:23

Lord, I desire to stay and live in that rested, refreshed place in You.

Recognize It's Me

When the roar of the crowd bids you to come, and the speed of the movement sucks you into a vacuum of momentum going the wrong direction, allow My voice to be louder. Stop. Breathe. Remember. Recognize that it is Me who goes before you. Submit and trust the pace of your life to Me. When you acknowledge that I know the plans for you, then you can willfully release the rhythms to Me. The going and the coming are in Me. The promotion is in My hands. As you step toward Me, your steps and your path becomes brighter and brighter. Learn to not only be able to turn around and look back and see how I have moved in your life, look forward and see Me directing you into destiny. Submit and trust Me. Watch and see what I will do.

Deuteronomy 31:8   *Jeremiah 29:11*
Proverbs 4:18

Lord, as I look ahead and not behind, You will cause my path to become brighter and brighter. I trust in following You.

Notice

Eyes are the windows to the soul, and there are empty eyes all around you. They reflect so perfectly what's in the heart. When I looked on a crowd My heart would beat with such compassion. They were so lonely, so broken, so lost. I set the lonely in family, your family. I have come to heal the broken hearted through you. I have come to save, not condemn, so the lost might be found with your help. All I ask of you this day is to notice. Notice the empty eyes and trust Me to help you show compassion—that compassion will be My heart and hands extended. Lay self and greed aside. Look up and take notice of those eyes looking back at you, waiting for you to respond. Step out. Be bold. I will show My compassion through You.

Matthew 14:14   Luke 4:18   John 20:21

Jesus, give me eyes to see what You see. Holy Spirit, teach me to move like You move. Use me, Lord.

Give Thanks

Slow down, open your eyes wide to see Me. Don't allow the fog of this world to blur your sight of Me. Clean the glass with thanksgiving and see what I reveal. In everything, giving thanks to Me is how your vision comes into focus. Saying thank you is not a magic word that makes troubles go away. In this world you will have troubles, but thanksgiving allows you the doorway to My presence, where together, we have the joy you long for. When you utter thanks to Me I see that you know who I am. It is then you realize that I am good and the giver of every good and perfect gift; then you slow down enough to know that I am your God. You giving thanks is proof to this world that you know Me and I know you as friend. Give thanks with a grateful heart.

1 Thessalonians 5:18   John 16:33

Psalm 138:1-4

God, You are good and I give You my thanks. You alone are worthy of all glory and praise.

Surrender The Load

A gentle reminder today that I am and will always be your strength. When you feel the heaviness of burdens and the weight of circumstances, I will once again ask you to give them to Me. When your heart is heavy and your shoulders feel tired, surrender the load and find rest. Fears and complications can be put to rest in My hands. Strength and peace walk hand in hand in My kingdom. My peace will always bring you strength and My strength will always bring you peace. So, today I infuse you with both of these so that My rest will be alive in you. Be engaged with rest. Allow heaviness to be swallowed up in My peace, knowing that I am always your present help in time of trouble.

2 Corinthians 12:9   John 14:27

Psalm 46:1

Lord, thank You for Your strength and Your peace. I receive this today and rest in You.

To The Finish

I have placed My hand on you and put eternity in your heart. Your walk with Me on this earth is not dependent on circumstances or pleasures. I have set plan and purpose before you to accomplish. Run this race with diligence to the finish. This is not a set of sprints to be run and then stopped. This is an endurance race of commitment that requires your all. Walking with Me is not something you try and see if it works for you. Walking with Me is a life surrendered and poured out to the finish. You will never walk alone. Even when you fall, I will pick you up. My desire for you is this: just as I was able to say "it is finished", I want you to say at the end of your life, "I have accomplished all the Lord had me do. It is finished". Keep walking.

Ecclesiastes 3:11

Hebrews 12:1-3

God, I choose to walk with You to the end. You set eternity in me. I will never walk alone.

Never Ending Circle

My eyes roam and look throughout the whole earth to find the ones I can show Myself strong in. I delight in giving My strength and blessing so that all can see and recognize My greatness. As you pour your life out for Me, I can pour My favor out on you. As you seek My face to do My will, I seek to meet your every need. As you take steps of faith toward My light, I shine brighter with faithful leading. When you open your mouth to speak, I will fill it with My words. As compassion comes from you to others, I will send forth grace and mercy to shower you. When you set your eyes on Me, I proclaim you the apple of My eye. We are in this together; I in you, you in Me, a never ending circle of love and power.

2 Chronicles 16:9 John 14:20

Psalm 17:8

Father, I love doing life with You!

Self-Serving Ways

Loving the unlovable; Blessing those who curse you; Forgiving undeserved actions; Giving what you don't have; Believing when you can't see. These and more are these places I want you to live in. None of these are done without My spirit living big in you. Nothing in this world's ways of selfishness will prepare or train you for My ways. Living a selfless life that is surrendered to My bidding takes a constant letting go of self-serving ways and thoughts. But I assure you that you are free to love and give your life to serving others. You can set your mind toward loving them because I have set My mind on loving you. Your rewards come from Me, not the appreciation of anyone else. I am the promoter. Love because I love you. Forgive because I forgive you. Give because I give to you. Believe because I believe in you.

Isaiah 55:8-9   Galatians 5:13
Matthew 6:3-6

Jesus, I desire my motives to be pure and selfless in all I do. Help me to do all I do as unto You and as You have done for me.

Your One Life

I see you lovely and whole. My eyes see your heart and the gifts I have placed there. I know you are tempted to compare yourself to others, but these comparisons will paralyze you. What I have placed in you to be cannot be compared to anyone else. You, My child, are wonderfully made. Everything about you, and even the seasons of life and how they change you, all this is in My hand. I gave you a life to live, don't lust for someone else's life. Don't allow your heart to seek for what another has. Your one life is yours. It is My gift. You are My gift. I gave you to be uniquely you to this world, for such a time as this. I gave you to all who come in contact with you. Rejoice and be glad. Live in the fullness of who I made you to be.

Psalm 139:14 Song of Songs 4:7

Father, I receive my life from You as a gift. Teach me to live it fully devoted and thankful to have it.

All Grows From The Small

I am shifting things in My spirit around you. I am quickening the day of destiny. I am placing things in order that will yield forth My harvest in your life. Make sure doubt does not take any root in you, for nothing is impossible for Me. The weed of doubt will choke the vision I have birthed in your heart. I alone know how and when to move and shift things into play. Be watchful and patient, for I am the one who brings promotion. Keep your heart pure and serve Me with gladness. I will and can open up windows in heaven and pour out My blessings. Despise not the small beginnings, for all grows from the small. Surrender to changes and the leading of My voice. Keep hands open to receive all that comes in My name.

Proverbs 29:18   _Psalm 100:2_

Zechariah 4:10

Father, keep my heart from doubt. Help me yield to the process of growth and time. Promotion comes from You.

A Banner of Love

My banner over you is love. You continually have a canopy of My complete, and everlasting love over you at all times. I never take this banner down. It does not fall if you fail. There is no darkness that hides it. There is no height or depth that can take it from you. My love banner over you is a covenant of unfailing and undying promise to love you always. Open the eyes of your spirit and see the ways I show My love to you. See what I see when I look at you. You are My child, called by My name, wonderfully made and saturated in My great love. Receive all I am and walk in all I have given you, knowing that every step you take there is a banner of My compassionate love over you, in you and working through you.

Song of Songs 2:4   Psalm 103:17

Psalm 136

Father, so great is your love for me that You have placed a banner over me called love! I love you.

Twists and Turns

This life is full of twists and turns. Surprises and unexpected events can send you into what feels like a whirlwind. Your plans sometimes go exactly as you thought they should and all stays calm. But as you look back through the times of uncertainty and chaos, you will find Me there growing you up, teaching you, and building your character. Your roots grow down deep to hold on tight in a storm. I am always with you. I never walk away. So, as you look forward, place your hand in Mine. I promise to not let go. And whenever a curve gets too sharp or a road too bumpy and you feel you won't make it, trust in the one who holds your hands. You are never alone. Hold tight to Me. I won't let you stumble.

Deuteronomy 8:2

Colossians 2:7   Psalm 23

Father, You always lead me. You never leave me. You are growing me to look like You. Thank You for loving me that much.

You

You are a gift. You are here for so many reasons; I placed you where you are for the benefit of all those around you. You are not here just to hoard a blessed life for yourself. Your life is a gift. You are the blessing. You will be the one who will help others find their destiny. You are the voice that will encourage and speak peace to troubled lives. I have not placed you here to think highly of yourself and sit in judgment of those not like you. I want to train you to see with My eyes, eyes of compassion and care. See with eyes of believing that fishermen can be great disciples. The ordinary made mighty. You are where you are to duplicate My life to others. Don't worry yourself over yourself. What you do for others, you have done into me. And great is your reward.

1 Thessalonians 5:11   2 Corinthians 13:11

Colossians 3:13   Romans 12:2

Father, help me be Your hands and feet. Not prideful and judgmental. Help me see others with the potential that You see in them.

Words

I am not a man, I do not lie. You can totally and completely trust My words to you. The promises I have made are secure and will not change. Words can be teasing and tempting, they can paint false pictures in your mind and lead you down paths of destruction. Twisted false beliefs can cause you to build your entire life believing lies. Empty words of flattery and false hopes build you up and then send you crashing down in disappointment, but My words are truth. My words give you life and hope. You can be fed and live and breathe by My words. The tongue can spread poison or give life and health. Learn My words. Watch your words to others. Be a life giver through your words. Life and death are in the power of the tongue.

Numbers 23:19   Psalm 119:50

Proverbs 18:21

Lord, help me watch my words to others. Help me put Your words in my heart so I can speak life to others.

Free

In this world situations and circumstances can wind chains around you. When you feel like a prisoner in a cell, when walls you have built inside seem high and thick. When others control your days and negative thoughts haunt your nights, and when oppression and depression can weigh you down and hold you captive; it is from all of this My child that I have come to set you free. I don't set you free for relief; I set you free for freedom. You are free in Me to walk in newness of life. Free from inside prison walls. Free from all that holds you. You are free to live. Free to hold your head high and walk with Me in sweet surrender. My life was so your life could be free.

Titus 2:14   Galatians 5:1

Jesus, thank You for giving Your life that I can be free. I am so grateful to You.

Our Time Is Always

I know you are busy and your mind is cluttered. I know you are having a hard time sorting out your time and how to spend it. Don't allow guilt and shame to take you to a place of feeling like a failure. Don't allow people to tell you how you are supposed to spend your time with Me. Our time together is always. I am not going to leave you just because you go to work. Our conversation is constant. I am always listening and always responding. You are My friend. I delight in you. I have promised to be with you and be your help. Every moment is our moment. Your mind may be crowded with many others that pull on you for your attention but always, always know I am here. I am closer than the mention of My name.

Psalm 73:28   James 4:8

Lord, thank You for Your nearness. I love knowing You are my constant companion.

No Fear In Me

So many fears sit in wait at the door of your mind. Fear that you won't be accepted. Fear you won't be good enough. Fear of being wrong. Fear of being rejected and pushed aside. Fear that nothing you say matters. Fear you won't succeed even if you try. Fear is the subtle enemy that takes hold of your thoughts and works its way into your actions. Fear always says "you won't" or "you can't". But I say "you will", and "you can". Over and over I say "do not fear", "do not be afraid". I have showered My love on you in a constant rain because My love will drown out all fears. Dance in the rain of My love and let Me saturate you and wash away the fears. Lock eyes with Me. See Me only. There is no fear in Me.

1 John 4:18   Isaiah 41:10

Father, thank You that I can walk free from all fear because of Your great love.

Giving and Receiving

Reach toward Me with hands open. I desire to fill your hands with gifts of My grace. Your hands open represent an open heart to receive. To all who will receive, to them I give. My giving never ends. Don't allow your hands and heart to close and clinch tight so that My gifts go by unnoticed. Keep your heart tender and your hands open wide. Seek with your eyes and find every gift given. I will daily load you down with blessings and cause goodness and mercy to follow you around. Those in your wake will sense My presence all around you. This place of openness with Me is found in our intimate times together. You pour out to Me, I pour into you; our perfect union, giving and receiving.

Luke 6:38   Psalm 68:19

Father, thank You that Your nature is to give and to receive. Teach me Your ways.

Finished Product

Keep your thoughts free from disappointment, it will blur your vision and cause you to lose hope. Don't forget that I am working to finish what I have started. When I begin a good work in someone they look like a lump of clay with no form at all. They may think they look like a finished product, but rest assured I am not finished yet. As I press and mold, twist and bend, My plan will unfold. Most of the time what a man thinks He is going to be is not what I had in mind. So I work. Steady turning. Steady molding. So rest in rejoicing over the process of time that I take to finish what I began. Look on each other with grace and patience. I am doing a good work.

Proverbs 29:18   Philippians 1:6

Isaiah 64:8

Father, I want to be what You want me to be. Finish Your work in me. I surrender.

Leading and Following

Trust Me with all your heart. I lead you toward green pastures, a place where you will be able to rest. As your shepherd I will guard the door so that no enemy gets to you. I will gather you up close to Me and protect you from evil. I will call you and you will know My voice and follow Me. Still waters of refreshing will restore your very soul within you as you walk with Me. Leading you is My responsibility, following Me is yours. If you can't see Me where you are and fear sets in, just listen and you will hear My voice calling you back to Me. And should you find yourself in a trap set by the enemy, call Me. I will leave the ninety-nine to free you. I love you that much.

Psalm 23   John 10:3   Luke 15:4

Lord, Your love is so kind and caring. You are so good to me. I love being Yours.

One Step At A Time

In quietness I gently move around you. I shift and shape and mold you. Even when you are totally unaware, I am working all things for your good. When your heart is beating in steady rhythm with Me and My will, My plan unfolds before you. Going before you is a path of light and love beckoning you forward. The river of My grace runs free to overflowing. Before you are doors and people that I have strategically placed for your good. As we walk together I will tell you what I see. I will speak to you in dreams and visions to reveal My purposes for you. Walk in My purposes for you, and you will find them revealed one step at a time. Each new day has My blessings, My plans, My purposes that are waiting for you.

Romans 8:28   Acts 2:17

Psalm 86:11

Lord, I choose to follow Your leading today. Show me Your ways. I know you are working for my good.

If You Are Listening

Listen to the sounds around you as you go through the day. You will hear if you are listening to the sound of the people's cries for hope. You will hear the silent desperation of longing and searching, reaching into empty space for answers that only exist in Me. You will see the chasm of emptiness in their eyes if you are looking. You will notice the ones that I draw you to. I will cause a yearning in your soul to bless and touch and speak. Speak out a word of encouragement. Give a light of hope. All need it; all need Me and more of Me. Some are sliding away from Me and just need a hand to lead them back. Be that hand, be the ears that listen. Be the mouth that speaks. You take the steps to do this and I will take it from there.

Galatians 5:22   Colossians 3:16
1 Corinthians 13

God, open my ears to listen to the hurt around me and teach me to respond like You.

Precious Moments

Eyes truly have not seen, nor ears heard what I have for those who love Me. I am in constant pursuit of your love. I am in constant motion to express to you how much I love you. I want you with Me for eternity, not just for a while. I prayed the price for you so you could come freely to Me. I love the sound of your voice when you say My name; it causes Me to say "ask whatever you want in My name!" I have much to give you and lavish on you. I love when you come close to Me in My presence and choose to just breathe in My love. I know in those precious moments you know I am your God. I love you; I desire your deepest love from your heart. You will be amazed at what you will hear and what I will show you.

1 Corinthians 2:9   Isaiah 64:4
John 14:13-14

God, I love my moments with You when I am made aware over and over again how amazing You are.

You Can't Run Out

I am giving you grace for this journey. I know your days seem hard and the nights are even longer, but I am promising you My grace is enough for you. Yes, you will doubt Me and you think you will fail but if you will hold tight to Me, we are going through to the other side of this tough time. My grace is always sufficient, more than you need. You can't run out. The supply is eternal. Never try to earn My grace, there is nothing you can do. There is no price you can pay. It is and will always be My gift to you. My gift that all you have to do is receive. There is a steady flow of grace that requires a steady open receiving. You can trust Me and you can trust My grace. I am with you. We will walk through together.

2 Corinthians 12:9   Ephesians 2:8

Galatians 1:15

God, thank You for Your never ending flow of grace toward me; it is always more than enough and it never runs out.

Divine Crossroads

Timing is everything, My timing is vital. Don't let the world push you. Listen for those door knobs to turn in people's hearts. You will be able to sense an opening of the heart and soul. Be cautious not to bust down doors and run through road blocks. My timing is everything. Be aware that the intricate workings of My spirit have strategically caused you to be where you are and with the ones you're with. I cross your paths in My timing. Be sensitive to My spirit. You will know if you are standing at one of these divine crossroads. If you are listening carefully to Me and to others these divine moments can change lives forever. Obedience is your part; changing people is Mine.

Isaiah 30:21   Ecclesiastes 3:11

Galatians 5:25

Lord, I want to walk in Your spirit and listen carefully to Your voice so that I never miss a divine moment You design for me.

Soul Rest

Come and rest. Set your eyes and mind on Me and simply rest. Allow Me to lift the heaviness and free your shoulders from the weight. Burdens are so heavy and cause your heart to lose hope. Lay the troubles in My hands and put your hope in Me. Quiet the negative self-talk and let Me fill you with confidence. My purposes for you have placed you where you are and I have placed in you all that you need to accomplish what I have planned. You will be the most productive when you are at rest in Me. When you let Me be your guide and your confidence, destiny will break forth. Trust Me with all that concerns you and let your soul rest in the promise that I am here and I am holding your hand.

Matthew 11:28   Proverbs 3:5

Psalm 130:7

Lord, You give rest for my soul. I receive the peace that trusting You brings me.

One Thing In Mind

When I placed you on My potter's wheel and wrapped My hands around you, I knew you in My mind. I could see the finish before the beginning. I knew destiny before birth. As you begin to yield away from hard stubborn will to a soft surrender, I begin. I smooth by adding the water of My spirit to baptize you in surrender. I shape and mold you by the words of My mouth and the works of My hands. When others come along and press in on you to reshape you, I still have My blueprint in mind and can form you back. If the enemy breaks you, I still have the salve to mend and restore. I had one thing in mind when I formed you; I only wanted a place to dwell. I am making a home for Myself a beautiful temple for Me. A place for My glory to rest in. you are My home.

Isaiah 64:8   Jeremiah 29:11

Isaiah 44:24   1 Corinthians 3:16

Lord, I am fashioned and made by Your hands to be Your dwelling place. Rest Your glory in me.

It's Yours

I am your supply. No supply ever runs out in Me. I am never short on anything you need. I am altogether delighted when you choose to receive from My abundance. It is pleasure for Me to see your heart open wide to My gifts. My storehouse is full to overflowing, so full that when the windows open My blessings pour out of them. Don't be caught in the lack of provision this world has for you. Nothing on earth can satisfy like Me. Draw from My storehouse. Plant in My kingdom garden and reap your harvest. Harvest comes to those who invest their lives in My wealth that is laid up for them. the riches of knowing Me and My ways will bring you to a peace in knowing that I am the all sufficient one and My storehouse is not only full, it's yours.

Philippians 4:19   Matthew 6:19-20

Malachi 3:10

Father, You are so good. You supply my every need. You are so much more than I can ever imagine.

Together

Champion one another's dreams and visions. I plant eternity in hearts and give dreams and visions to pull you to your destiny. Most will not go after My plan because they have no encouragement from others. I don't want you to encourage one another so you will feel better about yourself; I want you to encourage one another to march on. Believe in one another and help each other. Together you bring destiny into being. There is no large part or small part. All are equal in My plan. Press in together and let My life flow through you as a body, not just as individuals with separate tasks. Help one another and champion each other's callings in Me. Give yourselves whole-heartedly to be encouragers and watch how I will show My love to all.

Hebrews 10:24-25   Romans 1:12

1 Corinthians 12:27

Lord, help me be an encourager to everyone. We are all important to each other and we need each one to be whole.

My Peace

The unexpected can come quickly and sometimes cause your heart to fear. Don't be anxious or worry but turn your heart toward My love and let Me drive away the fear. Let the words of thanksgiving usher you into trusting Me completely. I will send guards of peace to shield your mind and your heart. My peace will hold you and keep you steady. Give your ears to My word and let my voice be your comfort. The enemy will speak lies that will be accompanied by fear. Do not open the door to them. Trust My peace to do what I have said it will do. Allow the guards of peace to protect your mind from anxiety. This is not the world's peace; this is My peace I give to you.

Philippians 4:6-9

Lord, You are my peace. Don't let me be fooled by the world's peace. I choose to walk in the peace that only You give me.

Nothing Compares

I am always here. I am ever present with you. While you are busy in your day, I am close to you. Take time to stop and let Me hold you for a moment. Let My presence embrace you and keep your mind at rest. I am here to listen and I will answer you when you call to Me. I want you to know how much I love being a part of everything in your life. Being with you is My delight. I spin around and sing My love songs over you. So as you go your way this day, know that I am with you. Know that I am for you. I want to cause your plans to succeed. I can promote and bring prosperity. But nothing can compare to the moments that I can embrace you and tell you how much I love you.

Psalm 139:18 Zephaniah 3:17

God, Your presence is so amazing. And Your love for me is so great. Thank You for always being with me and loving me so tenderly.

Very Secure God

Stay at rest, child. I promise not to change. So many things in your life change. People come in and out of your life. Friends are here today and gone tomorrow. I am a constant, faithful friend. I promise to never leave you or turn My back on you to forsake you. Children grow and move on away from you, but that is My plan. I want them to learn to rely on Me and not you. The seasons of your life shift and twist. They cause you to lean into Me and learn of Me. As you lean in close, you will find that I am steadfast and sure. As sure as the dawn breaks into a new day, My promises are forever settled and will not change. Embracing changes in this life may be very difficult at times; but you can be sure that I am your rock and your faithful, unchanging, very secure God.

James 1:17   Psalm 119:89

Lord, My only security is found in You. Thank You for being unchanging and steady.

Don't Waste Your Wanting

The desire to want more is of Me. The pressing forward and seeking destiny is a longing, I placed that in you. But the enemy of this world, the father of lies, has confused My people and caused the longings in their hearts to turn to greed. I placed in you a desire to want more of Me. I long to satisfy you at the very core of your heart, with all of My generous, overflowing goodness and love. I desire you to taste and see My goodness and allow that to cause you to dip deep into My wells of joy. I want your every step to be one of great anticipation, that an answered prayer or fulfilled promise is in your every moment. Don't waste your wanting on the things of this world. Don't chase after empty plans and dreams. Come to Me, I will give you My dreams to run toward and never leave you wanting for any good thing.

Psalm 23:1   1 John 2:17

Father, it is true, the more I seek You and taste of Your goodness, the more I want more of You.

Gather Your Seeds

This is a day to plant love in all you come in contact with. Today, sow My grace filled heart of love and acceptance wherever you go. Most do not understand My love. They don't know I love them with an unconditional love. The ground of their hearts can be very difficult to break through. The hurt and pain makes the soul dry and hard. Plow gently and slowly. Let the rains of kindness and grace soften and soak through the outer crust. Let your light shine on them so they see. If your light is too harsh it will blind and burn. Offer forgiveness and mercy for the hardening of the heart so it will open for the seeds of love to fall in and take root. Be watchful. For hurting, love hungry souls are all around you wearing masks of happiness. I will help you see behind the mask if you will be aware. Gather your seeds.

Colossians 3:12-14

Father, help me to clothe myself in all that You are. Live through me so others can know You.

My Name

I give you the gift of My name. It is the highest of towers that will make your heart glad. All will know My name and bend their knee to Me. You will be identified in many ways with Me. Peace will be manifested to all who know you because of My name. It will cause great favor to rest on you and clear a way that no man can accomplish. The very mention of My name can give you wisdom and restore brokenness in the deep wounds of the heart. Speak My name. Let My name be heard from your lips. It will allow others to know I am with you. In all of the vast meanings of My name you will find I am your all in all. Treasure awaits you in the mine of My name. Dig deep and know me. I am yours and you are Mine.

Philippians 2:9-10 John 14:13-14   Proverbs 18:10

Jesus, it is in Your name that we have power and safety. Teach me and show me the power of Your great name.

Peace On Earth

Peace on earth is what I came to give. My plan is for that peace to be in you so that it can manifest around you. All are searching for peace in their minds and in every part of their lives. You have that peace in Me. So don't allow this world and the circumstances of it to steal your peace. If yours is gone, who will they seek to find Me? Drenched in My peace, I can cause a calm and an assurance to rest on you that beams like the sun. I will attract the broken and hurting when you are My person of peace. Peace on earth begins when you open your arms wide. With boldness, step out and embrace contentment inside yourself. Give peace away not as the world gives, but as I have given.

Colossians 3:15   John 14:27   Isaiah 26:3

Father, I choose to receive Your peace. I will keep my mind on You and walk in Your peace. Use me to share Your peace to all I meet.

The Newness Of Now

Open your hands and let go. Turn loose of yesterday and all that was in it. Let go of hurts and offences that control your thoughts. Drop all the shame and guilt that clothe your mind. Dip into a fresh day's grace and mercy. Wash in the power of a cleansing stream. Never again will yesterday control tomorrow. The newness of now is a moment by moment embrace. Choose Me in every moment. Refreshing is flowing from Me to you at all times. I will send My word and revive you and cause you to be restored and whole. Open your hands to receive My fullness. There is no such thing as emptiness in Me. I fill to overflowing, running over abundance. Blessed is the one who trusts in Me.

Philippians 3:13   Jeremiah 17:7   Psalm 119:50

Lord, I desire to live in the fullness of every new moment. I will let the past go, embrace this day, and trust You with all my tomorrows.

Encounters With Me

I have over shadowed you with My presence this day. I am so close to you that fear must go and leave you at peace. There is nothing too hard for Me. Peace is here to guard you and your mind. I hold onto you when doubt makes you dizzy. I will not let you fall. In tribulation I am ever present. Doors of escape will open wide and allow you to be free from any snare the enemy sets for you. A refreshing balm of My goodness will bathe you, washing your eyes to see and know Me even stronger. There is a depth to My love drawing you into chambers with Me you have not yet even discovered. My hand will lead you to these encounters with Me that will captivate your heart and show you My love.

Jeremiah 32:27   Acts 3:19-20

Jeremiah 31:3

Lord, You have drawn me with Your great love and completely captivated my heart. Your love overwhelms me.

I Kept My Peace

Don't pass up a life of health and peace for stress and worry. My life of peace and My death were the perfect example for you to walk in. I had little or no money, no place to lay My head. People hated Me and said horrible things to Me. Men tried to stone Me and even throw Me off of cliffs. I have been spat on, My beard pulled out, beaten and crucified. Yet I trusted all the while in My father. I gave no worry about tomorrow but I prayed and heard His voice. In peace, I did what I heard Him say do, and said what I hear Him say to speak. It did not make My life free of pain, but I kept My peace and that is the same peace I give to you. Don't trade it for anything! It is worth more than gold; it is your very life's health.

Proverbs 4

Father, not only does Your word revive my spirit, it is health to my mind and my body. Your peace gives me health.